You Can Have It All

Also by Arnold M. Patent

Death, Taxes, and Other Illusions

You Can Have It All

Revised Edition

Arnold M. Patent

Celebration Publishing
Sylva, North Carolina

Celebration Publishing
Route 3, Box 365AA
Sylva, NC 28779

Cover design by Barbara Patent Anik

Composition and typesetting by Zapset, Los Angeles, California

Library of Congress Catalogue Card Number: 90-84993
ISBN: 0-9613663-4-6
Third Printing
Printed in the United States of America
Printed on recycled paper ✺

To my wife, Selma, whose love and
support prepared me to write this book, and whose
suggestions and editing brought it to life

Contents

Foreword

Tacked up on the wall facing me, where I write and work, is the Latin phrase *veritatis simplex oratio est*. Translated, it means truth is simple. I was reminded of this phrase when I first met Arnold Patent and became even more convinced of its message as I attended his workshop and experienced the way he teaches the simple but powerful truths and laws of life.

Here is a man who, after practicing real estate law successfully for many years, decided to change careers. Here is a man who does what he loves to do, does it superbly, and in doing it helps others do what they love to do.

As you read this book you will learn that you are the only one who determines the path your life takes. *You Can Have It All* is an excellent road map to lead you on a joyful journey.

JAMES BOLEN

San Francisco, California
June 1984

Preface

This book deals with the basic laws (principles) of the Universe. These principles have been recognized for many years, but relatively few people know them and even fewer use them in their daily lives. The purpose of this book is to acquaint the reader with these principles and then to describe ways in which they can be used to increase the quality of a person's life.

The principles are straightforward and easy to understand. Benefiting from them requires, first, a belief in their validity and, second, a clear intention to use them. This book describes the principles and explains simple ways to use them.

The material in each chapter is related to the material in every other chapter. Thus, reading the entire book will add to the understanding of each chapter.

To obtain maximum benefit from this book, I suggest that you reread it several times.

I have taken the liberty of alternating the use of male and female pronouns. Words synonymous with God are capitalized.

Acknowledgments

There are many people I wish to thank for their contributions to the publication of the original edition and of this new and revised edition:

Selma Bokor, Steve and Donna Schwartz, Jim Bolen, Theresa Czajkowska, Layne and Sandy Fant, and Katherine Hart.

Grady Claire Porter for generously sharing her meditations.

The coordinators of my workshops who invite me to their cities and the participants in the workshops and in the international network of support groups who continue to teach me so much and support me so generously.

Melva and Jesse Johnson, Joyce and Ivan Blostone, Katharine Deleot, Jean Crane, Toni and Gerry Hazlewood, Chuck Griffin, Ronnie Kerchal, Dr. Stanley Nelson, Lenny Levy, Tom and Bea Barabas, and Caroline and Marcus Goodkind for their immense contributions to the support group network.

A basic principle is that the Universe is a mutual support system. My preparation for writing this book and the direct support I received in bringing it to completion is a tribute to that system. I am fortunate that I have been trained to receive huge amounts of love and support by my family, who continue to shower it upon me. Expanding on that model makes the rest easy.

Preface to the Second Edition

More than six years have passed since I wrote the first edition of this book. Much has changed since then. The world has changed, I have changed, and my readers have changed. We are all experiencing the ever-expanding nature of life.

Universal principles, the focus of my book, do not change. However, their meaning to us—which derives from how we view them, how we interpret them, and how we use them—changes, as we do. Our broadened and expanded understanding of life has enabled us to see principles in an expanded light. I wish to share my expanded view of them in this second edition.

While much of the book remains the same, I am eager and happy to offer this new material.

You Can Have It All

Revised Edition

1
How It Started

Each morning when I woke up, I did exactly what I thought I was supposed to do. In practicing law, which I did for more than twenty five years, I struggled to deal with my clients' problems and with real estate investments. It is true that I earned enough money to live a model life in an affluent suburb of New York City, but what a price I paid!

The model life, instead of bringing me joy, brought only pain, which I carried with me all the time. Clinically, doctors found nothing wrong with me. Yet so great was my discomfort that I began to search for a way to make myself well.

I started by taking vitamins and changing my diet, but that didn't seem to help. With my focus on diet and vitamins, I came across a very sophisticated nutritional program that intrigued me, and I flew to Chicago to learn more about it. During four days of intensive study, I decided to go on the program. I took at least a hundred pills a day, including vitamins, supplements, digestive enzymes, glandular stimulants, and so forth. After a while, I noticed that I felt better, so I stayed on the program for a year and a half.

The most significant part of the program, though I didn't realize it at the time, was a daily regimen of meditation, based on the belief that stress is the single most destructive factor in one's life and that meditation is the single most effective and beneficial way to deal with it.

1

I immediately began meditating, and continued for the full year and a half that I remained on the program.

It was at this point that I discovered what were for me new ideas. What were these new thoughts that so fully captured my attention and my imagination? They were what I call the basic laws of the Universe. These are the principles, known for many, many years, that explain how the Universe works. They are simple, straightforward, and very easy to understand. However, since they are contrary to the teachings of our society, they are generally ignored.

Having learned how to accept challenges as a lawyer, investor, and businessman, I was now ready to undertake what seemed like my greatest challenge—adopting these principles as my day-to-day guidelines. And so began the second chapter of my life.

I applied the same perseverance to the practice of these principles that I had applied to the nutritional program and noticed even further improvement in the way I felt. By this time, the discomfort in my body was greatly reduced, yet I realized that I was far from rid of it. I began to appreciate how much pain I had experienced all these years. No wonder I had so often been uptight, jumpy, impatient, and unhappy.

When I started to follow the new thought program, I discontinued the nutritional program. Not only did I sustain the improvement I had achieved, but I continued to improve. The improvement has continued, with every indication that it will do so until every last bit of discomfort has been released from my body.

I began to share the ideas with others who were interested. I soon realized that my way of stating and explaining the principles was very clear and convincing, owing, in part, to my legal training and experience. After all, I had been trained to apply a body of legal principles to an endless variety of factual situations. What had changed was the body of principles.

In any event, I was encouraged to continue to present these ideas to others. Before I realized it, I had created a program utilizing many of these principles. This first program was a correspondence course offered to people in different parts of the country. A friend who was supportive of me as I expanded the program suggested that I offer a workshop to promote it. After leading my first workshop, I realized that I had found my ideal vehicle and outlet.

Starting with evening workshops that lasted about two and a half hours, I finally adopted a full weekend format: Friday evening, 7:00-10:30 P.M.; Saturday, 9:00 A.M.-6:00 P.M.; and Sunday, 10:00 A.M.-6:00 P.M.

These weekends have been so successful in demonstrating the power of mutual support, that I am organizing this book as I do the workshop to give you the opportunity of having a similar experience.

The Weekend Begins

Selection of the site is important. I favor a room that is light and airy, with space to conduct part of the program outdoors in mild weather. After registration, often with live music in the background, the workshop begins. The ages and backgrounds of the participants vary greatly, from six-month-old infants to eighty-year-old youngsters, with collars of all colors from white to blue and all those in between. College professors and academic dropouts, rich and poor, artisans and professionals, musicians and actors attend the workshops. It is exciting to watch this broad cross-section of people quickly and easily become a family for the weekend, freely offering support of all kinds to each other.

I start the formal part of the evening with a presentation of a number of the universal principles. Next, participants introduce themselves to people sitting near them. Later in the evening they join in six-person support groups. These groups meet several times during the weekend and offer the participants the opportunity to apply the ideas set forth at the seminar. By Saturday morning we are ready for the first of many question-and-answer periods, which help the participants learn how to use these principles to solve their personal problems.

Since I do not use notes, I rely on the needs, desires, and energies of the participants to direct me in the presentation of the materials. Though the basic material covered is the same, each workshop is unique in the ways it varies from its predecessors.

While the material is ostensibly presented from mind to mind, I like to ease its reception by offering live music and movement during the weekend. I suggest you take a similar approach. Please read small amounts between breaks. Listen to music, take a walk, or do some exercises every hour. To encourage you, I'll offer reminders.

Now we are ready for your private workshop to begin. Settle in your chair. Feel the energy of the others in the room, and realize that all of this material is natural to us. We just have to let go of our many beliefs that tell us that it is unnatural.

I usually start with the concept of energy.

2
Energy

Everything in the Universe is a form of energy. Energy occurs in two states—materialized and unmaterialized. The things we see around us, such as cars, houses, books, and trees, are examples of materialized energy. All energy that is not in materialized form comprises the balance of the energy in the Universe.

Both states of energy are more similar in form than appears to the naked eye. Even those objects that seem most solid, such as steel beams and concrete walls, appear as molecules in motion when viewed under high-power microscopes.

How does energy reach materialized form? It does so in a most surprisingly simple way—through the mechanism of thought. Whatever we see around us was at some prior time a thought. Another way to express this is to say that we create with our thoughts.

This places each of us in an extraordinarily powerful position. However, to benefit from this power, we must first believe we have the power, and then we must use it in beneficial ways.

What else do we know about energy? It is in infinite supply and available to everyone all the time. There is an Intelligence behind it, and it follows very definite laws.

We are influencing energy all the time, since we are thinking all the time. This is true whether or not we are consciously aware of our thoughts. Psychologists tell us that we have more than fifty thousand thoughts each day, and most of them are the same as the ones we had the day before.

The majority of our thoughts are in the form of thought structures or beliefs. These are our programs, our preconceived ideas for interpreting the world around us—the criteria or standards by which we decide how to function, how to behave, and how to react.

Most of our beliefs developed in our early years. When something occurred that seemed important to us, it generated a feeling response. The feeling was aroused by the nature of the event which caught our attention. If the occurrence was pleasant, such as a warm and loving hug, we interpreted it in a positive way and began the development of a belief—the connection of our interpretation of the event with the feeling that the occurrence aroused.

If the occurrence were a reprimand for something that we were doing, such as licking an ice cream cone while some of the ice cream dripped onto our shirt, we probably interpreted the occurrence in a negative way and began the development of another belief.

The difference between a random thought and a thought structure or belief is the difference between any random event and an event or experience that has meaning to us at a deep level of feeling. Our beliefs, which are really deep feeling experiences, determine the way we view the world. These beliefs are also responsible for the quality of our lives. When we expand our limited beliefs, we expand the quality of our lives.

The degree of importance each of our beliefs has for us is measured by the amount of feeling behind it. It is the feeling behind the belief that gives the belief its power.

In summary, then, we create the quality of our lives with our beliefs, which are energized by our feelings. Since there is no limit to what we can believe and feel, there is no limit to how joyful and abundant our life can be.

Alignment with the Universe

There are basically two ways to approach energy. We can either align with it or resist it. Alignment with it means accepting the natural way

6

in which the Universe functions and living our lives by the universal principles according to which it functions.

The process of alignment is one of accepting that which is natural to us. This means reperceiving many beliefs that we have adopted. These are the beliefs that cause us to interpret life in ways that lead us to struggle not only with the natural abundance all around us but with each other.

The process of alignment with the Universe includes opening ourselves to the Infinite Intelligence of the Universe. This Intelligence is available to each of us—in truth, It is a part of us. Accepting the fact that we have access to this Intelligence allows us to open ourselves to It. This Intelligence contacts us through our intuition. We feel It and hear It when our conscious minds are quiet and we are in a state of calmness and peacefulness.

Achieving a state of peacefulness and calmness is what life is really all about. It is through this state of being that we access all that we hold dear to us. It is in this state that we allow ourselves to feel love. Love is synonymous with the Universe. Love is the motivating force, the source of all power in the Universe. It is our willingness to be loving to ourselves and others that opens us to the true abundance of the Universe.

Love transforms everything. Universal principles are the simple guidelines that help us to find that love and to use it toward ourselves and with one another.

Let me suggest a mental picture to remind you of the infinite supply of energy—love—that is always available to you to create the quality of life that you desire. See yourself in a sandbox at an ocean beach. Your sandbox is filled with sand, and there are miles of sandy beach in three directions. You give out pails of sand from your sandbox to passersby. As your supply is depleted, you reach out and refill the box with the unlimited supply of sand that is all around you.

You may now be wondering, "When I am fearful, anxious, or angry, how can I achieve a state of peacefulness and open myself to this infinite supply of energy?"

In order to answer this question I must first introduce a thought about how the Universe works. The Universe is always on purpose (see chapter 4). And one of its purposes is to encourage each of us to follow Its principles.

This encouragement occurs in the form of signals. As we choose to live by universal principles, we experience the ease and grace of the universal supply of energy flowing through us. Conversely, when we select guidelines at variance with universal principles, we feel the struggle and effort of resisting the natural order.

Understanding our relationship to the Universe is essential to creating a peaceful interaction with it. And what is the Universe, this large Entity that is our home and of which we are all a part?

3
The Universe

The first step in understanding the basic principles of the Universe is knowing what the Universe is and how it functions. The Universe includes everything in existence from the smallest particle to the largest galaxy. Since everything in the Universe is an aspect of energy, the form any part of the Universe takes, or that all of It takes, is the result of thought (see chapter 2). The thought behind the Universe is called Infinite Intelligence, or God.

Infinite Intelligence is perfect, and thus the Universe and everything in It is perfect at all times. Human beings, as integral parts of the Universe are, therefore, perfect just the way they are. One of the hurdles that each of us must overcome is to believe this.

Infinite Intelligence is the life force, or essence, in everything we see in the Universe. Even apparently inanimate objects like rocks have essence. So it is with human beings. Each of us has an essence that is infinite and eternal.

One aspect of our essence is our conscious mind—our ability to think. We are free to think anything we wish. The quality of our thoughts determines the quality of our experiences. The more loving our thoughts are, the more joyful we feel, and the more abundance we allow into our lives.

There is no inherent limitation to our ability to make choices. Freedom invites exploration. This includes the freedom to choose to

9

create all kinds of individual and group chaos and crises. Exploration into all of the many ways we can frighten ourselves is one of the ways we, as humans, have exercised our freedom of choice.

Every choice has a consequence. By taking note of the consequences, we can decide to choose differently. When our exploration into fear has tired us sufficiently, we are ready to begin the journey back to peacefulness and joy.

There is constant motivation in everything to move in the direction of experiencing more of its own perfection. This is true of trees, plants, insects, and even minerals, as well as of human beings.

We know that the essence of one entity can contact another. Many of us talk to plants and animals. In fact, we are communicating with everything all the time and are receiving responses, even though we may have no conscious awareness of that communication. Communication takes place via the energy signals we emit, which are a result of our beliefs.

The way we interpret our experiences become our beliefs, and these beliefs determine the signals that we give out to everyone and everything. These signals generate experiences that are consistent with the signals. Thus, every belief of a positive nature will return a positive result, and every belief of a negative nature will return a negative result. Each will reflect the belief precisely in kind and quality (see chapter 16).

Most of us have been taught, or have interpreted our experiences in such a way as to believe, that life is not inherently a joyful and naturally abundant experience. As a result, we attract experiences that are consistent with such a belief. Since we tend to block awareness of most of our beliefs, attracting experiences that are consistent with these beliefs helps us to learn what these beliefs are. Beliefs that misperceive the truth do not change the truth. Not too many years ago, most people believed that the earth was flat. That belief was a misperception. It did not make the earth flat, but it did limit most people's mobility.

The Universe, created and kept in operation by Infinite Intelligence, continuously sends us signals to guide us in remembering who we really are and what life is really all about. These signals provide us with an incredible opportunity, for if we keep an awareness of them, we can function in support of ourselves and each other with total certainty all the time.

How do we pick up these signals? Through a mechanism that each of us has—our intuition. Intuition, which is Infinite Intelligence talking to us between our thoughts,* speaks softly. In order to hear It, and feel It, we must tune out the other mechanism—our conscious mind.

What are the signals? Basically, there are only two. When we are functioning in alignment with the Universe, we experience a sense of comfort in our bodies. When we are out of alignment, we experience discomfort. Another way of describing the signals is to say that when we are in harmony with the Universe, we are hearing with our hearts, and when we are out of harmony with the Universe, we are hearing only with our heads.

As infants, we function mostly on an intuitive basis. Since our rational society discourages the use of this mechanism, as we advance in age we are encouraged to disregard our intuition and to rely instead on our conscious mind. We are also encouraged to close our hearts.

Mastery of the intuitive experience, as with mastery of anything, requires a clear intention to master it. In order to develop that intention, we first question the belief that rational thinking is superior to intuition. Next, we must learn what our intuition feels like and what it sounds like. Then we must use it. We have to be able to distinguish the difference between intuition and something that seems like it, but is really our conscious mind talking.

Sometimes we have an investment in a particular result and therefore have no interest in listening to or following our intuition. Think of yourself as a third-year student at a university majoring in science. You realize that what you love to do is create graphic designs. In order to pick up the intuitive signals that will guide you in your choice of a career, you will have to let go of the perceived need to complete your course of study as a science major. Your intuition can still tell you to obtain your degree in science. However, you want to be certain that you are not influencing your choice by your vested interest in the three years you have already devoted to obtaining the science degree.

* This definition was given to me by my friend Phil Laut, author of *Money Is My Friend* (Cincinnati, Ohio: Trinity Publications, 1979).

Keep in mind that in order to improve the quality of your life, you must be totally honest with yourself at all times.

A useful and pleasurable way to experience your intuition is through artistic expression. Using color (crayons, paint, chalk, or pencils), allow yourself to express yourself without any conscious mind control. Choose your colors and designs intuitively. It is a fascinating experience and will tell you a lot about yourself.

Doing a series of these artistic renderings over a period of time, you will notice a continuity in your pictures. You will learn to trust yourself to express yourself freely. And you will get in touch with your intuition.

Similar creative expression can be done with music, dance, and sports. Allowing yourself to respond intuitively will help you learn what letting go feels like—another aspect of intuition. It will also teach you about trusting the inherent perfection of the Universe.

A simple and effective way to practice the principles is when you feel safe. Becoming comfortable with universal principles while playing tennis, painting, or dancing is no less valuable than in any other context. Pick the times and places that work best for you. Remember, the Universe supports you in keeping it simple and making it easy. Avoid waiting for crises to practice using the principles. Practice them when your life is peaceful, quiet, and comfortable.

After a topic is presented in the workshop, I ask for questions from the participants. I shall continue that format. Here are some of the questions I have been asked.

Question: How does the Universe create as compared with how we humans create?

Answer: All creation is a result of thought applied to energy or thought focusing energy. Every time a thought occurs, it influences energy. The more intention behind the thought, the greater the manifestation that results.

Every thought has some impact in the physical universe. Everything we experience in the physical universe is a result of a thought had by one or more people. Since everyone is capable of having any thought or combination of thoughts, the shape taken by the world around us, and all the experiences we have with it, is constantly changing. To the extent there is consistency in our thoughts, we discern patterns within our world.

Only the Universe, Infinite Intelligence, or God, creates what is real. What is real is the essence in everything. In humans, that essence is endowed with a conscious mind. Our essence knows everything. It uses this knowledge to guide us through our lives. Our essence does not make mistakes. The challenge facing each of us is to recognize this fact and then use it for our benefit.

Another way of approaching this is to see every situation as a lesson that the knowing part of us has arranged in order to teach us something that we need to learn. As soon as we learn it, we no longer need to face this kind of situation again. Until we learn it, we face it over and over again.

The simplest course for each of us to follow is to surrender our conscious-mind thought processes to Infinite Intelligence and to allow that perfection to express itself through us. It is when we surrender to that perfection that we understand what the true creative process is all about. It is then that we are free to express ourselves from our essence, which is who we really are.

Expressing freely is the state in which artists create magnificent paintings, musicians compose inspiring melodies, and ballplayers move with the grace and agility of ballet dancers.

Question:	I can see how the creative process works for the Michelangelos, the Beethovens, and the DiMaggios. But how does it work for the rest of us?
Answer:	The same way that it works for them. The principle is the same. What *seems* to be missing in us is creative

talent. Yet the difference between those people who freely express their creativity and the rest of us is only a perceptual difference. Those who do not express their creative talent believe either that they do not have it or that it isn't worth expressing, or have some similar limited belief about it. The truth is that everyone has at least one talent (see chapter 6) that is not only worthy of being expressed but that must be expressed for the individual to be at peace with himself and to feel a sense of fulfillment.

The talents each of us has are literally God given, and they are given to be expressed. Suppressing them requires effort, which is also a significant way we resist the natural order of the Universe and the abundance in it that is there for us to enjoy. We fail to express these talents at great cost to our physical and spiritual well-being.

The fact that society often discourages the free expression of our individual talents does not mean that these talents have no value to us or to society. In fact, the opposite is true.

The Universe, in Its infinite wisdom, does not create talents without the corresponding need in others to experience the expression of those talents. If a musician is inspired to express himself in a totally new musical form, there are people who will enjoy hearing music presented in this way. In truth, each of us is a potential Michelangelo, Beethoven, or DiMaggio in the area of our talent. We are each created to be a superstar. It is for each of us to locate that talent and then to express it. When we express it, we learn about its value in creating a life of fulfillment, abundance, and joy.

Question: You mentioned that our vested interests make it difficult for us to follow our intuition. Can you speak more about how our vested interests inhibit us?

14

Answer: Actually, the commitment to vested interests is all-pervasive in our society. Careful attention is required to notice the many ways that vested interests influence our thinking.

We see examples of vested interests when we look at the various segments of the workforce in our society. Each person—professional, clerk, salesperson, executive, or laborer—has a desire, usually on a subconscious level, to have her way of making a living continue. So her thoughts will tend to support that.

As a lawyer, I remember when no-fault insurance was introduced. My practice at that time did not include automobile negligence. At first, I thought I wasn't directly involved. It didn't take more than a few moments of additional thinking for me to ask myself this question, "What will those lawyers who can no longer support themselves with automobile negligence cases do?" I realized that many of them would branch out into real estate law, my specialty.

Though I perceived the threat that the proposed no-fault legislation posed for me personally, I also realized that the concept of the legislation was beneficial to the community. Society deserved the benefit of this improved thinking on the subject of insurance. I was prepared to support it. I noticed, however, that some members of my profession started publishing articles and other materials explaining all the ways in which the new legislation was inadequate. I sensed that these arguments were not being offered to support the public; rather, they were justifications for preserving the status quo, intended to discredit this new legislation because it was perceived by lawyers as threatening to their vested interests.

The concept of vested interest is important for you as the reader of this book. You may have a vested interest in thoughts, ideas, and concepts that are totally at variance with many of the thoughts, ideas,

15

and concepts expressed in this book. You will have to remain continually vigilant to notice the subtle ways in which you might resist even considering the value of these concepts.

Our next topic, which was introduced, in part, in chapter 2, is the concept of purpose. I mentioned that the Universe is always on purpose. Yet most of us haven't ever thought about *our* purpose. It is now time to think about it.

4
Purpose

There is no more important step you can take than to define your life's purpose. It is the answer to the question "What is your individual role in the Universe?" You must become aware of your role in order to benefit fully from the beauty, the power, and the perfection of our magnificent Universe. You can become aware of this role by defining your purpose.

Your purpose develops your sense of belonging to our Universe. It establishes you as an essential part of this larger experience. You no longer feel the separation from your Source. When you define your purpose, anything that happens to you, viewed within the context of your purpose, appears meaningful and not as an isolated event in your life.

I suggest that you read your purpose at least once every day to reinforce your awareness of your importance in our Universe and to help you keep your channel open to the Source of all energy and the Source of all guidance in every decision you are called upon to make.

I also suggest that you read your purpose whenever something is troubling you. The troubling event or circumstance is perceived as troubling because it is viewed as an isolated event in your life. Seen against the backdrop of your purpose, the troubling event changes in your perception of it as well as in its effect on you.

Defining Your Purpose

1. List one or two of your unique personal qualities, such as *enthusiasm* or *creativity*.

2. List one or two ways you enjoy expressing these qualities when interacting with others, such as *supporting* or *inspiring*.

3. Assume the world is perfect right now. What does it look like? How is everyone interacting with everyone else? What does it feel like? This is a statement *in the present tense*, describing an ultimate condition, the perfect world, as you see it and feel it. Remember, a perfect world is a wonderful place in which to be.

    NOTE: Define your purpose as though it is presently happening, not as something that will come into being after certain preconditions are met.

    Combine the three numbered items into a single statement.

    EXAMPLE: My purpose is using my creativity and enthusiasm to support and inspire others as we all freely express our talents in joyfulness, harmony, and love.

Joy Attracts Fulfillment

Part of the perfection of the Universe is that it provides the motivating factor and the energy to create a life of ever-increasing joy. This allows you to fashion a life of such beauty that you cannot wait for the next day to begin.

There are just a few preparations that you need to take to accomplish this, as follows:

Carefully define your purpose and keep it uppermost in your mind by reading it at least once every day. Develop a sense of the value of your role in the Universe.

Have your life become an expression of your doing what you love. This is the specific way that you express who you really are. You are now fulfilling your perfect role in the universal scheme. You will feel yourself as part of a winning team, with each play of the game a wonderful challenge and opportunity. Since the game doesn't end, you can't ever lose. You simply improve your skills and enjoy the benefit of steady improvement.

Continually remind yourself of the real game and play it as often as possible. When you are living your life in alignment with your purpose and doing what you love, you are automatically playing the real game. Reinforce your focus on the real game by reading books that inspire you to continue playing your role in even more fulfilling ways.

View every experience from the context of your purpose and in accordance with universal principles. This improves your ability to feel peaceful under all circumstances.

Be part of a support system that is devoted to playing the real game (see chapter 42).

The Inspiration of Purpose

If there is no purpose in your life, why live it? When you have a purpose, you invite inspiration into your life. You express your real self. What joy this releases!

Question: Can you suggest other ways in which my purpose can be used on a day by day basis?

Answer: Purpose has many uses. In fact, it is basic to many things we do. If we ask ourselves how what we are about to do aligns with our purpose, we can greatly simplify and improve the quality of our lives. An event has either little or great meaning depending upon how we see it in relation to our purpose. We can see everything we do in the context of our purpose. This leads us to eliminate certain things that we do and to see other things that we do in ways that give us greater satisfaction.

Another thought about purpose: Whenever you consider joining with either one or more persons—whether in a business, a social group, a common-interest group, or a personal relationship—it is most important to define your purpose for coming together before you make any commitments to the group.

A simple and effective way to deal with purpose when considering a venture involving two or more persons is as follows:

Each person defines his individual purpose.

Each person compares his individual purpose with that of each of the other members of the group.

Each person defines the group purpose.

Each person compares his definition of group purpose with that of each other person.

The group creates a simple statement of group purpose that inspires all the participants. Take the time that is required to develop a group purpose that will inspire each and every participant. Unless a participant is inspired by the group purpose, there is no point in his being a part of the group. Lack of alignment in purpose will eventually surface, probably when the group is least eager to deal with it (see chapter 41).

Life can be a liberating experience—an opportunity to express who we really are. We can make peace with and then release the part of ourselves that wants to struggle, compete, and suffer.

The simplest way to liberate ourselves is to view life from the highest vantage point. It is only by seeing life in universal terms that we feel inspired to participate in inspiring ways. Having a purpose, and feeling the inner need to express that purpose, is essential to having a life of truly high quality.

If there is one concept that is central to the mastery of the other principles and to understanding how the Universe functions, it is the concept of perfection. In order to use this principle successfully, we must be willing to relinquish the belief that perfection is either fanciful or unrealistic.

5
Perfection

Perfection describes the way in which the Universe functions. It is a marvelous principle that helps us to see all aspects of our lives from the highest vantage point.

What are some of the indications that the Universe functions perfectly? The sun furnishes just the right amount of energy to support life and it does so without depleting its own supply of energy. The earth rotates on its axis with total precision, and without any wear and tear on itself. Our planet is supplied with the perfect balance of gases in the atmosphere to support life. Each of us has the ability to perform functions beyond human understanding, naturally and effortlessly: We secrete chemicals to digest food; we make instant complex calculations necessary to chase and catch a fly ball; and we combine two cells to create another human being. We do all of these things and many more with no conscious-mind control of the process.

By using the highest thought, as in using the principle of perfection, we guarantee that everything and everyone we deal with will be treated in the best possible way.

How can you use this principle of perfection in your daily life, moment by moment? Believe that you and everyone else is perfect just the way you are, and treat yourself and everyone else as perfect just the way you are. For example, a friend has just been fired and she stops by your house on her way home. She appears angry, upset, annoyed, and fearful. You can notice how she is acting and accept these actions as real, or you can look beyond them. You can realize that how she is acting is an expression of her beliefs at this moment; that behind these beliefs is a perfect human being who is capable of experiencing her perfection at any moment that she recognizes and believes that she is perfect just the way she is.

You can listen to her without supporting her belief in her anger and fear. You can just continue to see her as perfect. Without support for her negative beliefs about herself and her situation, she will be encouraged to reperceive them. The result achieved will depend, at least in part, on your ability to convey a real belief in her perfection just the way she is.

An interesting fact about the concept of perfection is that it is available only to those who use it. Ignorance of the concept or an unwillingness to believe in perfection deprives one of its benefits. Conversely, those who believe in the concept receive the benefits of it.

It is impossible for us to live our lives in a vacuum. We require some touchstones to guide us. Each of us uses standards, guidelines, and criteria in the conduct of our lives and for the decisions that we continually make. Every experience we have is the result of the use of these standards, guidelines, and criteria. Put another way, whatever we believe determines the results we achieve; how we view events and people determines how we experience them.

How, then, do we create a higher-quality life experience? One of the most effective ways is to adopt the principle of perfection. Use it as the standard and reperceive all other beliefs in terms of a belief in perfection. As long as we require some standard for our behavior, why not choose the one that gives us the most beneficial results? The higher the thought or principle that we use, the closer we come to total alignment with the Universe.

Belief in perfection encourages us to function on an intuitive basis. Using our intuition is listening to Infinite Intelligence. When we use our intuition, we must relinquish use of our conscious minds. Bypassing our conscious minds releases all blocks in the flow of energy around and through us. The result is a feeling of aliveness, the experience of perfection.

Question:	Since everyone is free to act any way he wishes, why should we not honor the way a person expresses himself to us, be it anger, sadness, or confusion? Why look for the perfection behind it?
Answer:	It is always a matter of having the quality of life that *we* truly desire. The way to improve the quality of *our* lives, if that is what we wish, is to see a situation from a higher thought level. This is what we do when we view a situation in the context of a universal principle.

Connecting with the essence of the person behind the anger or other emotion that is being expressed is a choice that we always have (see chapter 15). It is a decision in favor of playing the real game. It is also the answer to the question "Which game is more fun?"

Question:	Why is it that we human beings who were created perfectly function with such apparent disregard for each other's perfection?
Answer:	It is a result of free will. I made up a story to explain the way I see it.

God, or whatever It is you believe in, was almost finished with Her creation of the Universe and was down to the last detail. She called a meeting of Her board of advisors to decide one final issue. Here was a perfect Universe all ready for creation. The human beings, so integral a part of it, were incomplete. How should they be completed? Was the perfection of the Universe such that everyone had to live a life that was perfect in the ideal sense, without any choice? Or was the human being to be given a choice in the matter? After some deliberation, the board of advisors decided that the Universe would be much more interesting if humans had a choice about how to live their lives. And so the concept of free will or free choice was born.

To give validity to the concept, a vehicle had to be created so that free will could be exercised. Thus, the conscious mind was created. It remains, paradoxically, the greatest tool and the greatest source of mischief in existence.

Being totally free, we can see things any way we like. Believing, as most people do, that our individual intelligence and group intelligence is extraordinary, we are continually tempted to create life experiences that are based on so-called rational thought processes. Fortunately for us all, many people are now questioning that choice. They are at least considering the advantages of using free will to subordinate their conscious minds to Infinite Intelligence. This allows the inner creativity and talent that each of us has to flower into full and free expression as an integral part of the perfect Universe.

It is only our ego selves that keep motivating us to try to re-create with our limited intelligence a Universe that has already been created perfectly. We can see and feel that perfection in ourselves and others whenever we are willing.

One of the ways the Universe has chosen to express Its perfection is through Its gift to each of us of one or more talents. Being in touch with and expressing these talents is a key to releasing our inner joyfulness.

6
Doing What We Love

As described in the previous chapter, the Universe and everything in It is perfect. One aspect of that perfection is that each of us has been given one or more talents. When we express these talents, we are carrying out our roles in the overall plan of the Universe.

The Universe supports Itself by encouraging each of us to fully and freely express our talents. When we do what we love, we are encouraged by a feeling of comfort in our bodies. When we avoid doing what we love, we experience discomfort.

We do not learn a talent—it is a gift of the Universe, and each talent comes complete with the tools to express it perfectly. For example, if we have an artistic talent, we have all the skills necessary to express that art form successfully. However, we must want to express it, delight in practicing it, and share the joy of its expression. By practicing it consistently, we uncover more of our talent and gain confidence and comfort in expressing it more fully and freely. We also give ourselves the remarkable pleasure of honing and refining the talent through consistent expression.

It is a process of surrendering ourselves to the Universe and allowing It to play through us.

Expressing a talent is not a conscious-mind experience. As artists and musicians, we do not think about what colors or notes to select. We let go of any sense of limitation. We become totally intuitive and allow the infinite supply of creative energy to flow freely through us. It is an experience of freedom and joy, not of thought and effort.

When we release all limitations, extraordinary things happen, and it is a different and unique experience for each person. When we are expressing our talents fully and freely, we feel our perfection. If we could take a pill that would release all our negative thoughts and open us to the Universe and Its infinite supply of energy, we would be able to express ourselves with total magnificence. In fact, we can do it as soon as we are ready. And the purpose of this book is to move us in that direction. We shall fly into joy whenever we are ready to untie our wings.

In summary, doing what we love is our way of supporting the Universe. The Universe in turn gives us total support and encourages us to continue.

The way we locate the particular talent that is perfect for us at any specific time in our lives is to look at what we love to do. For what we love to do is what we have a natural talent to do. The two are really one and the same. Doing the following exercise will put you in touch with what you love to do right now.

Discovering What You Love to Do

Make a list of the things you thoroughly enjoy doing. Limit the list to those activities that inspire you at the mere thought of them. The shorter the list, the easier it is to reach the desired result.

Select the item on the list that is most important to you. Do this no matter how much you may resist picking one item. Picking one does not mean that you have to give up doing the others forever.

Make a list of the ways you can express the talent that you selected in the second step. It is best to do this daily. Keep a separate book for this exercise. Do not judge the ideas that come to you as you do this exercise. Write down every idea that flows through your mind, no matter how silly or meaningless it may seem. The purpose of the exercise is to stimulate your creative mind. After doing the exercise for a period of time, you will have developed a habit pattern that will continually produce creative ways to express what you love to do.

The number of ways you can express yourself by doing what you love has no limit. Using your creativity to produce these ideas is one way to experience the abundance of the Universe.

We all know what it is we love to do. It is an integral part of us. We can, however, keep the information from our conscious minds, thereby failing to improve the quality of our lives. The pleasure from doing what we love is a deep, fulfilling pleasure. It is an expression of who we really are, our reason for being.

Question: Why must I pick one item? I love so many things that I can't bear the thought of not focusing attention on all the others also.

Answer: It is important to select only one item. This relates to the efficient use of energy. The more we focus energy, the more powerful is its impact. When we focus all our attention on one talent, we take advantage of this principle. Once we achieve a success that is satisfying, we can introduce a second talent, and so on.

There are many multitalented people. The ones who are successful started by focusing their attention on one talent. By allocating part of our attention to each of several talents, we scatter our energies and make it almost impossible to enjoy any of our talents at a high level of success.

Remember, each of us is a superstar when we lead from strength. Our strength is our talent.

If we look at the life of a recognized superstar, we notice that most of the things he does are very ordinary. He is perceived as a superstar because of one thing that he does extremely well. We all have a natural ability to do at least one thing on a superstar level. When we locate what it is, and do it as though the quality of our life depends upon it, each of us becomes a superstar also.

If there is one principle that raises more questions and has more built-in resistance to its acceptance than any other, it is the law of cause and effect. Acceptance of this principle brings with it the realization that we are not at the command of circumstances and the choices of others. This realization releases incredible energy to support us in improving the quality of our lives. Mastery of the law of cause and effect is a key principle in understanding how the Universe works and how our lives work.

I suggest that you take plenty of time with this chapter. It is important that you feel comfortable with the thoughts expressed in it. In fact, until you are willing to accept these ideas, it will be impossible for you to benefit from them.

7
Cause and Effect

This principle states that the knowing part of us, the part that is connected to Infinite Intelligence, creates the events in our lives. There is no such thing as an accident or a random event. And nothing that happens is the fault of anyone.

Furthermore, we are each volunteers who have agreed to enter into the precise circumstances that we find ourselves. Some of the circumstances we find ourselves in are very intense and very challenging. For example, some of us find ourselves struggling to pay our bills, others find ourselves unable to stay in a mutually supportive relationship, and still others find ourselves battling serious illnesses. Many of us have come to our present challenging circumstances from childhood experiences that were equally challenging, such as extreme poverty, child abuse, divorce, and alcoholism.

Our agreement to enter into the particular circumstances that we find ourselves is very purposeful: We have come to transform the beliefs, patterns, and feelings that have both given rise to and grown out of these circumstances.

We can be sure that whatever our circumstances, we are equal to the challenge. However, we need to be aware that we are not facing the challenge alone. We are all in this together. At our deepest levels we are all connected and we are here to support each other.

The Universe is a mutual support system. And although we have avoided following this model in the past, we are now ready to avail ourselves of it. The growth of support groups of all kinds is evidence of both our need for each other's support and our recognition that this support works. In fact, we are now learning that when we join together in mutal support, there is no limit to our accomplishments.

Any event can be a source of separation or an opportunity for a demonstration of love and mutual support. When we are willing to expand our vision enough to see and feel an event that we previously viewed in terms of victim and perpetrator as an opportunity to reach out with kindness and caring, we become vehicles for transformation of consciousness.

Our willingness to reperceive our beliefs about victims and perpetrators has another most important advantage. It enables us to reclaim our personal power, which we surrendered to our belief that we are powerless—victims waiting to be victimized by parents, employers, government officials, or just random events such as automobile collisions, diseases, and earthquakes.

Once we have reclaimed our personal power, it becomes available to us to bring peacefulness and unconditional love to every circumstance of our life.

Wanting Debts

For those of us who are challenged by debts, it is helpful to know that we took on the beliefs, patterns, and feelings of a debt consciousness so that we can transform them. And we have a substantial task, for our society is experiencing an expansion of its debt consciousness. Personal debts and city, state, and federal debts are at an all-time high and climbing.

To understand the concept of debt, it is helpful to see it as an outgrowth of the extensive reliance of our society on the concept of obligation. We were raised to believe that we are obligated to do many things—pay attention to parents, attend school, obey laws, earn a living, and pay taxes. So much of our life is devoted to things we do out of a sense of obligation that we have developed a strong obligation consciousness. Debt is just another word for obligation.

The many debts we create as individuals and as citizens are just an outplaying of our obligation consciousness.

Having immersed ourselves in the beliefs, patterns, and feelings of an extensive debt consciousness, we are in the perfect position to transform them. In fact, it is only through our willingness to take on the full intensity of these beliefs, patterns, and feelings, as well as the intensity of the circumstances that accompany them, that we can transform these beliefs, patterns, and feelings.

We carry out the transformation of our debt consciousness by first of all reminding ourselves, over and over again, that this is our purpose. When we have accepted this purpose, we then practice seeing and feeling the perfection of each and every debt and obligation that comes into our experience. Next, we do the Feeling Exercise (chapter 29) and continue doing it daily until we feel at peace with each debt and with each creditor. The resolution of the debt will emerge from our peaceful feelings about the debt and the creditor. The resolution can come about in many ways, including the funds to pay it, or a forgiveness by the creditor.

The discomfort that we feel from having unpaid debts is the signal to proceed wtih the resolution. When we avoid seeking this resolution, the discomfort intensifies, for our energy flows into our beliefs and feelings all of the time, whether we are consciously aware of these beliefs and feelings or not. And this steady flow of energy keeps intensifying whatever is going on.

The opposite of avoidance is awareness (chapter 27). Avoidance intensifies our discomfort. Awareness encourages us to bring ourselves into harmony with our environment.

There are times when we feel we are faced with an unexpected event that is very dramatic and very extreme. However, a careful examination will usually uncover many less dramatic experiences that preceded it and in fact forecast it. The Universe is a consummate teacher. It teaches us patiently, deliberately, and with absolute consistency. Even when we choose not to pay attention to a lesson, the teaching continues. Many of us have elected not to pay attention to many of these lessons. The signals were clear, but we chose to disregard them. Then one day we are faced with a dramatic event, which is just an advanced lesson in a series of lessons that we had been ignoring.

The solution is to remain aware of what it is that we have created. This reveals to us our underlying beliefs. Then we can reperceive those beliefs that are at variance with universal principles. Seeing and feeling the perfection in each event instead of judging it, blaming someone, or feeling helpless, puts us in touch with our personal power and inspires us to see and feel more of the perfection in even more challenging events. Seeing and feeling the perfection in each event also serves to remind us that we are in this together, and that through mutual support, there is no limit to how much we can improve the quality of our lives.

Question: If we always receive what we want, then how do you account for people who are killed in plane crashes?

Answer: One of the issues raised by the question is the assumption that death of the physical body is bad. The most relevant information we have on that subject comes from people who have had what are called near-death experiences. The consensus from the thousands of people who have reported on these experiences is that life without a physical body is wonderful.

In view of this consensus, is it reasonable to conclude that a person who chose to make that transition was in error? There are reasons to stay and reasons to leave. No one can make that decision for another. No one can really understand the reason for another's choice. Using traditional explanations, such as "He was in the prime of his life, in good health, and had everything to live for" cannot stand up against deeply personal reasons known only to the inner self of the person and that relate to the larger issue of the purpose of this lifetime in terms of the growth and expansion of consciousness.

I have an observation based on years of experience with many people: Those who believe in the law of cause and effect and use it experience remarkable improvement in the quality of their lives. These people say, "Yes, I have the power and ability to interpret my experiences in a way that improves the quality of my life."

My observation also discloses that those who focus on extreme situations and perceive them as exceptions to the law of cause and effect are the very people who avoid reclaiming their personal power and then using it to improve the quality of their lives. They are the ones whose lives do not improve in any significant way.

For those who still have doubts about the law of cause and effect, I have the following suggestion. Just assume that it does apply. There is no way that you can hurt yourself, for if the law does exist, you gain the benefit of believing it; if it doesn't, you lose nothing.

Not accepting the law of cause and effect means that you are at the mercy of events and can be a victim at any time. This encourages you to remain powerless. If you test the validity of the law, at least you know you have given yourself the chance to reclaim your power and use it to improve the quality of your life.

This is a good time to take a break.

The next topic is one that is a lot of fun to explain. Much of what we are involved with on a day-to-day basis involves this concept. And much of the confusion in our lives is a result of our misperception of it. So I introduce the concept of illusion, a concept not solely the domain of the magician.

8
Illusions

The world as we currently experience it is a result of a general agreement that things really are the way we think they are. Yet most of these beliefs are no more accurate than earlier beliefs that the earth is flat or that the sun rotates around the earth.

Not many years ago almost everyone believed these ideas. But such beliefs did not induce the sun to rotate around the earth. Today we find that most people believe that inflation is inevitable, calories affect weight, jails curb crime, politicians are unreliable, and armaments create national safety. These beliefs are also illusions.

How do we tell the difference between what is real and what is an illusion? An illusion is something that can change from time to time. What is real is always present.

Our essence is always present. Beneath the overlays of doubts, fears, and other emotions, we shall always find the real self, which is pure love. Any time we look for it in ourselves or in others, it will be there.

How, then, do we master the world of illusion? We withdraw our energy from it. Illusions continue to exist because people put energy into them. Inflation is kept alive because we think about it continually. So much energy is put into it that it must expand. This is true of any illusion. When energy is taken away from an illusion, it disintegrates.

All illusions rely on thought to focus energy into them to keep them alive. The thought can be on the conscious or subconscious level. Thoughts and beliefs that we are not even consciously aware of are responsible for keeping alive many of the illusions that we experience as reality.

Whether there is common agreement or not, it is possible for anyone at any time to release an illusion. This will happen when the illusion is recognized for what it really is. When the first person recognized that the earth was not flat and saw the illusion, it no longer controlled him. People who believe there is no relationship between inflation and their standard of living continue to live better on less money.

Let's examine the concept of debt as an example of how to deal with an illusion. Debts exist only because the concept is given general acceptance and is used extensively in our society. Car loans, home mortgages, and charge accounts are considered valuable vehicles for circulating money in our economy. Yet there are people who do not believe in debts, and they do not have any. Debt is not a requirement for living. Every day there are people who buy cars and houses for cash and enjoy doing it.

Debts are not a general condition. They are a specific condition. No matter how much difficulty we are having with cash flow, we do pay some of our bills. We do manage to handle money to some extent, and whatever that extent is, it is not an accident. We benefit those people we want to benefit and we withhold from others. What, then, is the procedure to master debts?

Make a note of all the assets you have and of all the abundance in your life. Make it a habit to acknowledge and give thanks for everything you already have. Remember, what you focus your thought on expands (see chapters 14 and 20).

Expand your concept of debt. When you receive something that requires repayment, such as a loan, think of it as a gift to you. When you repay it, see it as a gift to the original giver.

If you notice difficulty in repaying a particular creditor, realize that you want to withhold from him. Do the Feeling Exercise (chapter 29) until you are at peace with your feelings about your creditor.

Your peaceful feelings will support a peaceful resolution of the debt.

Question: What can I expect when I release my belief in an illusion but others around me continue believing in it?

Answer: This question points up two aspects of our lives. We function as individuals, experiencing life consistent with our personal beliefs. We also function as part of a society that contains many groups. Each one of these groups has beliefs. When the individual and group differ in their beliefs, the result is interesting.

To simplify the answer, it is possible for an individual to experience serenity and peacefulness in the midst of chaos. The more chaotic the group experience, the more deeply must the individual have mastered peacefulness and serenity.

Although each individual can achieve peacefulness on his own, the impact from the world around us is always felt. We can mute the impact by the level of our personal consciousness, but we cannot totally avoid it, nor should we be able to do so. Since we are all connected at the deepest levels of our beings, we are sensitive to the energy vibrations of everyone. Whenever the quality of someone's life improves, his energy vibrates at a higher level and each of us picks this up, even though we are not consciously aware of it. Of course, the opposite is also true. Whenever anyone experiences more pain, each of us picks up this lower vibration. The composite of all of our vibrations determines the overall quality of life on the planet.

For example: You have been annoyed at a friend for breaking a date at the last minute. At your support group meeting you ask for support in consciousness to feel forgiveness for your friend. Through the loving support of the group, you are able to feel forgiveness for your friend. Not only are you vibrating at a higher level, but so are the participants in the support group who have volunteered to be part of the experience.

As your life becomes more peaceful (a result of which is that your vibrational level increases), the higher vibrational energy signals that you emit are picked up as comforting and supportive by those whose energy fields are denser. This serves to encourage them to reach for higher vibrational levels within themselves even though they may not be aware they are doing so.

We are all seeing and feeling the demonstration of this process in the sudden and unexplained toppling of the Berlin Wall, the transformation of many of the communist societies, and the expanding integration of the European countries into a new community. These events are a direct outgrowth of the steady increase in the number of people on the planet who are yearning for peace, as witnessed by the growing numbers of those who meditate together for peace each December 31st.

So our role is always dual—to improve the quality of our own consciousness and to support others who seek to improve the quality of their consciousness.

Many of the principles involve paradoxes. The next concept is one of these. The paradox of this principle is that to truly have something, we must release all attachment to it.

9
Nonattachment

Air moves freely through the atmosphere. Water flows freely down rivers and streams. Waves roll freely onto beaches. The earth moves freely on its axis. So it is with the affairs of humans. Allowing things to flow freely in our lives gives us the maximum benefit from each experience.

Looking at it from the viewpoint of energy, we know that energy requires free movement in order to function effectively and efficiently. The energy of the Universe wants to flow freely through us. When it does, it benefits us and all who come in contact with us. Whenever we interfere with this free flow of energy, we reduce, proportionately, the abundance that we experience. Blocking the flow of energy also results in discomfort in our bodies—a signal from the Universe that we are out of alignment.

One of the ways that we interfere with the free flow of energy is by holding on to what we already have. We hold on to money or other things of material value. We hold on to people with whom we have a relationship.

Holding on to anything—people or things with material value—blocks the free flow of energy around our experience with the person or object and reduces the pleasure of the experience. It also inhibits the free movement of new things and new people into our lives.

Having Does Not Require Holding

There is a difference between having something and holding on to it. You can own a house, enjoy it, and feel no attachment to it. Or you can own a house, feel that it belongs to you, and that if you give it up you are losing something. The latter is attachment. It is a blocking of the free flow of energy into your life.

You can have a relationship with a person, feel a total commitment to the relationship, trust the other person completely, and yet have no attachment to the person or to the relationship. You give the other person total freedom at all times. The relationship continues as a result of the moment by moment recommitment of the participants to the relationship.

By not holding on to a relationship, you have an opportunity to allow other people to come into your life. Each relationship has its own kind of commitment that is special to it, and the experience of each relationship adds to the quality of other relationships. In fact, while we are experiencing any particular relationship, the energies of our other relationships flow through us to enrich our present experience. If we feel a need to hold on to one or more of our relationships, we block the free flow of energy around all of our relationships.

People tend to hold on to things or to accumulate them when they feel that they might not have what they need at some future time. In other words, they do not trust the natural abundance of the Universe to provide them with the appropriate things at the perfect time. When we do not trust the Universe to function perfectly, it reciprocates. It continually gives us what we believe, whether that be shortage or abundance.

Holding on to things is also a result of our belief that we know what it is that we need better than the Universe does. It is based on our assumption that the Universe is less than abundant and appropriately supportive at all times. Trusting the Universe to function perfectly at all times is a key to having the benefit of that perfection.

If each of us would put more of what we own into circulation, how much more there would be for everyone to share and enjoy. Remember that an infinite supply of energy remains available to everyone at all times. The only shortage we ever experience is as a result of our belief that something is in short supply or not available to us. What we are dealing with is a perception of shortage, not a real shortage. To prove this to yourself, think of any instance when you received something that you wanted without any effort on your part, just because you wanted it.

Mastering nonattachment requires the willingness to believe that the Universe is a place of abundance. Until we arrive at that belief, we create circumstances that validate what we do believe. When we finally recognize that abundance is our natural state of being, we release all attachments to our material abundance and then it flows freely into our lives.

Security—Trusting the Universe

The concept of nonattachment brings up the issue of security. How do we experience security? The one way we do not experience security is by collecting or accumulating assets. Security is not something that we attain outside of ourselves. In fact, the person who looks to create a feeling of security by amassing material wealth is missing the whole point. Security is a feeling that comes from trusting the Universe, believing that It functions in a way that is naturally supportive of everyone. Every time we choose to create a feeling of security by increasing our net worth, we are treating an illusion as real. We are expressing disbelief in our true security, which comes only from trust in the inherent safety and abundance of the Universe.

Question: To master nonattachment, is it necessary to give up all our assets and everything we own?

Answer: No. Having something and owning it in the real sense are two different things. We cannot truly own anything in the Universe. Nothing really belongs to us.

There is common agreement in our society on various forms of ownership, such as titles to houses and cars. We are led to believe that we can own things, and in fact we are encouraged to think that we own them.

43

Most of us were taught that success means owner-ship of many things. This overlooks the universal principle that no one can own anything. The only way to truly enjoy anything is to let go of it. If you notice that something stays around, then you know that it is perfect for you to experience it and enjoy it. If it leaves, you know something else is perfect for you to experi-ence at this time.

Letting go in order to have is an important concept. It requires a lot of practice. Letting go does not mean that we have to divest ourselves of everything. It is strictly perceptual. It means letting go of the perceived need to keep or own any or all of our assets. We can practice releasing attachment to things until it really does not make any difference what, if anything, we own. One of the major benefits of reaching this state is that we will not be disappointed or feel loss when the item is gone.

This brings us back to the principle of abundance. When we believe in it, we know that no matter what we give up, there is an infinite supply of energy available to replace it. It's an inspiring game—this game of universal principles. Everyone who plays it is a winner. It is the best and only real game in town.

44

10
The Mirror Principle

One way to view life is to see ourselves in a classroom. Everything that happens is just a lesson for us to learn. This classroom is quite different from a traditional one with walls, designated times of attendance, and rules and regulations that apply to the time spent there.

This larger classroom encompasses every place we go, everyone we interact with, and it is not limited by traditional measurements of time.

This all-encompassing classroom was designed as the most efficient and effective way of teaching us who we are and what life is all about. Since no part of our life is excluded, there is no place to hide or play hookey. Wherever we are, we are in this classroom.

There is a dynamic principle that applies in this classroom: *Everything that happens to anyone is reflecting an experience that the person is having with himself. Everyone and everything else is there only to give him a chance to more fully experience himself. Whatever feeling is being expressed is always his own feeling. This is true even though it might seem that another person is having or contributing to or causing the feeling.*

The sooner a person recognizes this principle and then starts to use it for his benefit, the sooner life begins to make sense, and the sooner he starts to gain some insight into who he really is.

I call this principle the mirror principle. For if we see ourselves surrounded by mirrors at all times, we realize that whatever is going on is just a reflection of ourselves back to us, so that we can see ourselves more clearly.

I view the Universe as the ultimate teacher. It teaches us directly and with total clarity. The mirror principle is the closest I can come to describe how this universal teaching system works.

As we grapple with the next concept and the principle behind it, we find ourselves also grappling with the concept of illusion. It seems so clear to us that when we give something away we no longer have it. How does this align with the principle that we give only to ourselves?

11
Giving and Receiving

The concept of giving and receiving is central to our understanding of abundance and other concepts such as illusion and energy. Giving and receiving are two sides of the same coin. To have a completed gift there must be a giver who truly wants to give and a receiver who wants to receive. The giver, after giving, creates a vacuum, in a sense, and is now ready to receive, and the recipient is in a position to give. It is not necessary that the receiver give something back to the same person who gave to her. The ideal is for both giver and receiver to keep the flow going and allow everything to move freely in and out of their lives. Holding on to anything, developing an attachment to it, blocks the flow.

Visualize a circle of people with each person giving to and receiving from another person in the circle. When one person holds on to anything, it stops the flow in the entire circle, and everyone in the circle feels the block in the energy. When everything is moving freely around the room, everyone receives the benefit of what is circulating, as well as the energy, which is circulating also.

We Give Only to Ourselves

There is a principle underlying the concept of giving and receiving that further encourages giving freely to others. The principle is that we give only to ourselves. Remember, we are always dealing with energy, which is in infinite supply. Giving energy to another person does not deplete our own supply. We can take in all the energy that we desire, all the time.

The energy flowing through us when we do what we love generates many gifts. The happiness we feel when we do what we love is a gift we give to ourselves. It also attracts the people who enjoy being around us, and who are eager to support us in all ways, including purchasing our products and using our services. It also encourages people to give to us just for the pleasure of giving.

To understand the concept of giving and receiving, it is important to define the term "giving." A true giving, or gift, fulfills the following conditions:

> The giver sincerely wishes the recipient to have and enjoy the gift.

> The gift is something the recipient wishes to have.

> There are no ulterior motives or strings attached by the giver.

When we give something for the pure pleasure of giving, and for the creation of an equivalent feeling in the recipient, we have a true gift. The return gift can come from any source, not necessarily from the original recipient.

When we appreciate receiving a gift from another, it sets up an energy that stimulates us to give. The more pleasure we feel in giving, the more energy we create in others for them to give. These are the dynamics behind the principle that we give only to ourselves.

Think for a moment of anyone you know or knew who enjoyed giving so much that she was the continual recipient of gifts from others. Many of us know such people. Each of us can become such a person when we integrate in our consciousness the principle that we give only to ourselves.

Taken to its ultimate, what are we really giving when we make a true gift? We are giving love, something that is in infinite supply, and something that is the motivating force behind the infinite supply of universal energy. Love truly makes the world go 'round. And as with everything circular, it keeps returning.

Question: How can I best use the concept of giving and receiving to obtain repayment of a loan when the debtor is resisting repayment?

Answer: Giving with strings attached, which is what a loan is, can result in almost anything. To the extent that you are attached to the money, the Universe supports you in learning to let go. The discomfort you experience is the Universe's way of telling you that what you set up is out of alignment with universal principles.

The simplest way to obtain repayment of a loan, if you are ever going to receive it, is to allow the borrower to take full responsibility for the debt. As long as you keep reminding her of the debt, she is encouraged to let the repayment be your responsibility. You can give the responsibility to the borrower and say, "It is up to you to decide what you want to do about the money you received from me."

If she ever had the intention to repay you, she is now in a frame of mind to feel that intention again. It is your best chance for repayment. Of course, the less you are concerned about whether she ever repays you, the more you set in motion the energy for others, not just the borrower, to give to you. Remember, the easiest way to have is to let go of the perceived need to have.

49

12
Details

The Universe handles the details. This is another principle that appears to contradict common teachings.

Handling details is generally considered a conscious-mind experience. It is usually an attempt to figure out the best way to approach a situation, or to plan how to achieve an objective. However, the conscious mind does not know all of the variables in any situation. Only Infinite Intelligence has this knowledge. As we relinquish this function to Infinite Intelligence, things will fall into place for us perfectly. Following our intuition—our connection with Infinite Intelligence—provides us with the perfect signals, or guidance, without any effort on our part.

For example, each of us at some time has had the experience of going to a place because it felt right to go there. What seemed like a chance meeting turned out to be a valuable connection. Looking back on it, we can see that there is no way that we could have planned the meeting, since the existence of the other person wasn't even known to us.

Allowing the Universe to handle the details is not a license to resign from active participation in life. Quite the contrary, it encourages active participation. When we look to the Universe for guidance for the most appropriate next step, we then proceed with certainty and are confident of receiving benefit from the experience. Following this guidance increases the flow of energy in and around us and makes participation in life more interesting and more fun, as well as more productive.

The statement that the Universe handles the details does not mean that It handles the details that we assign to It. When we align with the Universe—live our lives according to universal principles—we notice that the Universe handles details in a way that is truly supportive of us. Receiving this support encourages us to continue. When we use criteria other than universal principles, we are on our own. We must then handle our own details.

There is another way in which details are handled perfectly for us and for everyone else. The Universe is so perfectly conceived that when each of us does what he loves, all necessary tasks are performed as an expression of our love for what we are doing. This system creates products and services of the highest quality and supports us in doing what we love with confidence and joy.

The Universe Handles the Details

I can illustrate the concept that the Universe handles the details by relating a personal experience. One evening in 1982, I gave a preview of a workshop at an apartment in New York City. A woman attended whom I did not meet that evening. She left early and did not have a chance to introduce herself. She later told me that she was impressed with my presentation and made a mental note to ask me to offer a workshop for an organization to which she belonged. About six months later, I received a call from Patricia Horan requesting that I lead that workshop. I agreed.

After meeting her, I learned that Ms. Horan is a writer. She told me that she would like to write a story about me for a magazine for which she was a contributing editor. A few months later, James Bolen, publisher of *New Realities*, called. He decided to feature me as the cover story in his magazine. This total stranger, living on the opposite coast, introduced me to a wonderful new audience.

At no time during this entire period did I try to reach this result. The Universe, in Its infinite wisdom, handled every detail of it. Though it is now many years later, I am still in awe at the sequence of events and how perfectly they were handled.

Question: Are you saying that planning is a waste of time?

Answer: Yes. If we believe that the Universe is a place of perfection where everything has already been worked out perfectly, then our role is not to figure things out, which is all that planning is.

Thinking that life is a struggle, that unless we figure things out we will not understand what to do, are just thoughts we make up. The fact that many people think this way does not make it true.

We can, at any time, surrender to the perfection of the Universe and allow Infinite Intelligence to guide us on our perfect path. The only precondition to this is the willingness to believe that the Universe functions in this way. Try it! There is no other way to find out.

Question: Do you mean to say that I can live my life totally without planning?

Answer: Let me answer that by giving an example. Assume you start your day by creating a plan for it. You decide that at 9:00 A.M. you will have a meeting with Lucy and at noon you will have a business lunch with Harry and Mike. After your 9:00 A.M. meeting, the phone rings. It is your friend Fred. He tells you that he has just met Sam, a person who is an expert in your field and who has a wonderful contact for you in your business. Sam will be leaving town in a couple of hours, but he'd like to have lunch with you. Do you follow your preconceived plan for the day? Or do you have lunch with Sam?

The truth is that the Universe gives us signals every moment. If we listen and follow Its guidance, our lives work perfectly. As you can see, this is a radical departure from how we are taught to live and plan our lives. In fact, we need not plan at all.

It's important to realize that, from our vantage point

in the world of illusion, we can see only certain variables, options, or possibilities from which to choose. From the vantage point of Infinite Intelligence, all variables can be seen. If we just ask, the answer to which variable is best for us will be sent to us through our intuition, our connection with Infinite Intelligence. In the example just given, when the day was planned, you did not know that this wonderful contact even existed. How could you have possibly planned to meet him?

We all know how exhilarating it is to have spontaneous experiences. The traditional approach of our society invariably squelches opportunities for spontaneity. Trusting the perfection, the abundance, and the supportive nature of our Universe encourages us to let It handle the details for us. This, in turn, allows us to enjoy the spontaneity that comes from that trust.

There are times when it is appropriate to make future arrangements. When the time comes, we have an intuitive sense to do so. Our intuition in the present tells us to do something in the future. That is not planning in the traditional sense.

Question: Can you suggest what I might do on a typical morning after I awaken to prepare for my day?

Answer: First, clear your mind by meditating (see chapter 38). Then do the Feeling Exercise, which helps you to focus on the quality of feeling that you want to experience during the day (see chapter 29).

Remember, we attract to us those people and events that are consistent with the energy signals we emit. When we are feeling peaceful, we attract to us people and events that will sustain us in remaining peaceful. Starting our day in this simple way encourages such a result.

If you notice that you are unable to achieve a feeling of peacefulness, I suggest that you not leave home until you do.

Feeling peaceful before you walk out of the house, no matter how long it takes, is the best investment in time and energy that you can possibly make. Leaving home feeling depressed, confused, or anxious guarantees that your experiences during the day will be consistent with those feelings and will just serve to reinforce and very likely intensify them.

13
There Is No Right and Wrong

Our rational society has taught us to judge or evaluate virtually everything that we experience. So ingrained is this training that we feel incomplete when we haven't processed each experience in this way. Yet judging or evaluating anyone inhibits our ability to respond to the real self of that person. Each person is not the sum of her thoughts and actions. She is her essence, which is always perfect.

Locking In Energy

Once we evaluate or judge anyone or anything, these limited thoughts attach to our feelings about the person or the experience. This attachment of a thought to a feeling creates an energy block that causes us discomfort. We are then literally stuck in an experience the way we perceive it. Until we let go of our judgment of an experience, it remains the way we perceive it, and it continues to cause us discomfort.

The universal principle involved here is that there is no such thing as right or wrong, good or bad. Everything that occurs is just another event. By judging something, it becomes for us the way we judge it. The only way to experience the inherent perfection of anything is to see and feel the perfection of it just the way it is.

57

Let's consider the following example: You cut your finger. If you view it as a bad event and become angry at yourself for your carelessness, you miss the whole point. The fact that your finger hurts when you cut it is wonderful. This clear signal from the Universe enables you to keep your fingers intact. The pain also tells you that there is a part of you (obviously on a subconscious level) that is self-destructive. The knowing part of you is calling this to your attention to encourage you to become more aware of your self-destructive tendency.

Having our awareness heightened is most important, for until we are aware of something, we leave it the way it is. The signal of pain, which is really the knowing part of us giving us a strong signal to pay attention, can be used in many self-supportive ways. For example, we can ask for support in consciousness, at support group meetings, to pay more attention to the ways we do and do not support ourself. Inviting the group's support will make it easier for us to focus our attention on self support (chapters 40 and 42).

For another example, we can do the Feeling Exercise (chapter 29) as a way of going beyond the pain, beyond the beliefs and patterns that created the pain, to the underlying feeling. The underlying feeling holds the key to the resolution of any self-destructive tendency we have. It works this way: When we feel the feeling free of the beliefs we have connected to the feeling, we free the energy that is bound up in the feeling. It is the bound-up energy that we feel as pain.

The beliefs we hold are typically the interpretations we made of events that occurred in our life, usually at an early age. Many of these interpretations were that a particular behavior by a parent or other authority figure was not unconditionally loving and supportive. For example, we were crying in our crib because we were wet and uncomfortable and our mother and father, who had friends visiting at the time and didn't want to be disturbed, told us to be quiet instead of changing our diaper.

As very sensitive feeling beings in our early years, we readily interpreted many actions by our parents and other authority figures as unloving, and we felt hurt by what we interpreted as uncaring or even intentionally pain-inflicting behavior. Most of us are still

58

carrying this hurt as anger. And there is a part of us that wants to get even before we are willing to give up the anger.

What we didn't realize at the time we made the interpretations, and what those of us who are still angry don't realize yet, is that anger is always self-directed, even though we think it is directed at another. Each person can only feel and be affected by his own anger. The only way the person at whom you direct your anger can feel it is if it triggers his own anger at himself.

The solution for the judgments we hold of another is to begin feeling forgiveness, and to regularly continue feeling forgiveness until the angers, resentments, and desires for retaliation have abated. We then deepen the feeling of forgiveness until we begin to feel love for the person. We then focus on the love so that it can expand into deep love. You can use this same forgiveness process for any judgments you hold about yourself in connection with this person.

Concurrently, we do the Feeling Exercise (chapter 29) which, by opening up the energy around our feelings, makes it easier for us to release the angers and resentments, and reach the deep love that is always there. We can never escape from the fact that we are all deeply loving beings whose greatest joy and most natural way of relating is to feel and express deep love in support of each other.

It is also important to be aware that our true power resides in our feelings, and that when we allow ourselves to open to our feelings (which are all loving), we access this power and it becomes available to support us and provide abundance for us in more ways than we can possibly imagine.

Question: Do you mean to say that as an abused child it is not accurate for me to see the times when I was abused as bad and the times when I was not abused as good? They seem like opposites to me.

Answer: I understand that the presence and absence of abuse can appear to you as opposites—one bad and the other good. However, they are two sides of the same coin, two aspects of the same event. If they were opposites, then you would feel different when the event is absent from how you feel when it is present. But you feel the same way for both—angry. So it is not the stopping of the abuse that ends the anger. It is your willingness to see the event as perfect just the way it was, and to forgive the abuser.

Also, if your interpretation is accurate, then it would follow that during the times when you were not being abused, you should have felt peaceful and content. But this is not true. You were just as angry at the person who abused you during the times between the abuses. In fact, if you still see the abuse as bad, you are still angry.

As hard as it might be for you to see it, the variable that determines how you feel is not the presence or absence of the event (in this case the abuse), but your interpretation of it. It will be easier for you to be forgiving and release the anger if you can see yourself as a volunteer who came into this precise family configuration so that you could, by immersing yourself into these beliefs and patterns, transform them by accepting them as perfect just the way they are (see chapter 13).

The anger you feel has several origins. When you first came into your family, you began taking on the existing family anger along with their beliefs and patterns. You also took on anger when you realized that you had to give up your environment of unconditional love and nurturing support, as well as your innocence, peacefulness, and freedom to fully, freely, and spontaneously express how you felt.

So your anger predates the abuse, is purposeful, and since it is always self-directed, it is in your own best interest to proceed with forgiveness for the abuser and continue until you feel love not only for the abuser, but also for yourself. And keep reminding yourself that you are not a victim. You are an agent for transformation of consciousness. Also, reach out for all of the support you can obtain. When you open to support, you are helping to transform energy which had previously been channeled into abuse into mutual support.

Question: Since you do not believe in right or wrong, how should we deal with criminals?

Answer: One of the reasons our criminal justice system is so chaotic is that it is based on the assumption that there are such standards as right and wrong. When people do something wrong, as defined by our legal system, they are often punished.

Belief in right and wrong negates the principle of cause and effect. If the knowing part of me sets up everything that happens to me, how can I accuse anyone of doing anything to me?

Society takes what appears to be the easy way out. In fact, it is the hard way. Learning to accept the discomfort that we experience in our lives is easier in the long run than making believe that our discomfort is someone else's fault.

Saying there is no right and wrong is not saying that there are no consequences for our actions. Once we move past the concept of blame, we can then focus on what is really happening. If a person steals from or injures another person, even though the recipient wanted exactly what he received, the so-called perpetrator sets in motion certain consequences for herself. There is a mechanism within the perpetrator that handles it perfectly. She cannot avoid it.

When anyone inflicts pain on another person, or for that matter on anything in the Universe, the consequences are direct. The performer of such an act immediately feels discomfort. Though she may numb herself to the awareness of it, the pain will remain until she replaces the less than loving thoughts and acts with loving ones.

The law of cause and effect and the companion principle that nothing is right or wrong encourages us to see the perfection in everything just the way it is. Criminals have to learn that *they* can improve the quality of their lives. Society is not to blame, nor is a parent, sibling, policeman, or judge. A criminal who is sent to jail is not a victim of a bad criminal justice system.

The law of cause and effect tells us that we are neither victims nor victimizers. Every event in our lives is something that the inner knower of each of us creates so that we may have that precise experience. Eventually we learn that we are capable of seeing and feeling the perfection in every experience we have, particularly ones that we previously thought were unacceptable. When we remove the standard of right and wrong and substitute the standard of seeing the perfection in everything, the stage is set for the quality of everyone's life to improve dramatically.

The willingness to give up the standard of right and wrong is only the first step for a person who previously saw herself or another as a victim. Next comes the willingness to forgive, and finally the willingness to love unconditionally the so-called perpetrator. Until a person reaches the final step, there is no real appreciation for the power of love to heal and to create an environment of peacefulness and safety.

It is time for a break. When you come back we'll talk about a topic close to the hearts and pockets of most of us—money and material wealth.

14
Abundance

When dealing with money or any other aspect of the material world, the highest thought that we can use is the principle of abundance. The highest thought always includes and encompasses all lesser thoughts. Using the highest thought enables us to relate to everyone and everything in a most harmonious manner.

Abundance Is Our Natural State

What do we know about abundance? It is the natural state of the Universe. To have abundance in our lives requires a willingness to recognize that it is always available; we need only open ourselves to receive it. Stated another way, to experience less than total abundance in each and every aspect of our lives, we must actively resist abundance.

An example of resisting is believing that abundance is achieved by holding a job we do not enjoy but that pays well. Many of us assume that to earn as much money as we would like to have, we must do work that we do not like. The unhappy result of this belief follows from a misperception of the basic principle involved.

How do we use the principle of abundance to our benefit?

First, we must remind ourselves that abundance is the natural state of affairs in the Universe, and if we are experiencing less than total abundance in each and every aspect of our lives, we are actively resisting that abundance. Believing this precept is an essential starting place. Such beliefs as that we have to earn a living, be productive, achieve a particular life-style, gain credentials, or work hard are contrary to the principle of abundance. We must marshal great intention and commitment to integrate this new concept into our consciousness, since it is so contrary to our existing beliefs.

Second, we must become aware that our inner knowing has led us to our present experiences. This knowing part of us is using the challenges we face as the most appropriate way of helping us to make peace with the very people and circumstances that we view as unacceptable and intolerable.

Third, we must avail ourselves of the principle of nonjudgment. Whatever we believe and whatever we are doing is perfect just the way it is. Whatever anyone else believes and whatever anyone else is doing is also perfect just the way it is. Releasing judgment frees the energy around any situation and allows us to interact with others in ways that are mutually supportive and harmonious.

When we start to integrate these three steps into our consciousness, we begin to notice a feeling of peacefulness. As we continue to integrate them, our peacefulness expands.

Peacefulness is the door through which we gain access to the abundance of the Universe. As long as these concepts remain only an intellectual exercise, no real change occurs. Peacefulness heralds change. It is the signal that we have moved our beliefs from our heads to our hearts. Peacefulness also opens us to the infinite supply of energy that we were blocking. The flow of this energy through us creates a feeling of aliveness. This aliveness influences the energy signals that we emit and attracts the people and circumstances that will support the continuation of our feeling of aliveness.

Energy and Abundance

Since everything in the Universe is energy, abundance is also an expression of energy. Mastery of energy is mastery of abundance. It works as follows: When we do what we love because we love to do it, we channel energy into the creation of high-quality products and high-quality services. The people whom we attract are the ones who will buy our products or use our services and will be happy to pay us well for them.

Just think of owning an automobile that is built by a mechanic who loves to build automobiles. He selects and installs each part with care. The finished product is his pride and joy. Who would not consider it a privilege to own such an automobile?

The amount of energy we allow to flow through us is related to our willingness to do what we love and love what we are doing. The more we allow ourselves to express fully and freely, the more energy we allow to flow through us, and the more abundance we experience (see chapter 6).

Recognizing Our Present Abundance

There is another aspect of abundance. Much of the abundance that we think we desire we already have. Take our bodies, for example. They are extraordinary instruments with literally unlimited potential. Whatever we believe our bodies are capable of doing, they can do. We limit them only by our limited beliefs about their capabilities.

Most of us enjoy a remarkable array of abundance: caring and loving friends to spend time with, nourishing food to eat, wardrobes of clothes to choose from, comfortable housing to live in, a wide variety of transportation for all kinds of travel, entertaining and inspiring books to read, pets to comfort us, and flowers to brighten our day. The tendency, however, is to take for granted what we already have and to focus on what we do not have.

Whatever We Think About Expands

This leads us to another basic principle: Whatever we think about expands. By noticing the abundance that we already have, we open ourselves to receive more. By noticing what we do not have, we attract more scarcity. Use of this principle is illustrated by the following example. Assume that you have $100.00 cash in your pocket and $500.00 in debts. Most people tend to worry a great deal about their debts, and this causes the debts to expand. By appreciating the $100.00, and making peace with the debts and with your creditors, the $100.00 will expand. Feeling grateful for the $100.00 reminds us of the natural abundance of the Universe. In this frame of mind we are more likely to express what it is we love to do, which in turn will attract to us those people who will respond supportively.

Gratitude

Our focus on the $100.00 in our pocket is also a reminder of the many gifts that we have already received from the Universe. Feeling gratitude for all that we presently have opens us to receive even more.

Debts and Gifts

We can reperceive our negative concepts about debt by viewing it from its positive aspect. Debt is not the beginning of a transaction. It is invariably the second part. The first part involves receiving something of value, such as money, clothes, a car, a television set, a vacation, or a house.

It is beneficial to see the payment of the debt as a gift to the company or person who gave something to us. It is fun to give. When we give a birthday present to a friend, we feel good. Paying a debt can be similar. When it isn't fun to pay a bill, it means that we wish to withhold love. This leads us to expand our view of the creditor. As our thoughts about the creditor improve, so does the flow of money to pay the bill.

Again, I caution you not to be fooled by the basic simplicity of this idea. It is not only simple, it works. When we enjoy paying bills, and this includes paying taxes, we know that we are achieving mastery of the principle of abundance.

All of life is meant to be fun. When it isn't, we are withholding love from others and from ourselves.

Question: If abundance is our natural state, why do so many people struggle to achieve it?

Answer: When our belief is that we have to struggle to attain certain things, particularly material wealth, then the only way we shall achieve material wealth is by struggling.

I was just such a believer. During twenty-five years of earning a living, I achieved most of my material wealth in less than 5 percent of the time I devoted to my career. The rest of the time I literally created problems and obstacles that I had to overcome, so that the ultimate, successful result would be properly earned.

After I made the shift to doing what I loved, I blocked the flow of money. What I didn't realize was that I still had struggle and material success wired together. When I replaced the need to struggle with the fun of doing what I loved, I also eliminated financial success, which was still connected to struggle. Finally, I allowed fun and financial success to join together.

The principle that we always create what is perfect for us to experience cannot be pushed aside or avoided. It is in constant operation whether we pay attention to it or not. People who struggle for a living, disliking what they are doing, believe that their life cannot be an experience of ease and simplicity.

As rational and logical as most of us think we are, many of us still limit ourselves in an irrational way. We adhere to a superstitious belief that, in order to have some things in our lives that are good and positive, we must be willing to accept other things that are bad or negative. This belief in some mythical balance creates a continual impediment to progressing in any real way with the quality of our lives. We keep asking ourselves, "Is improving some aspect of our lives worth an unknown price we are certain we shall have to pay?"

Most of us are unaware of yet a further way in which

we block abundance. We fail to realize that the rate of flow of abundance we allow into our lives invariably reflects how we are faring with the core issues in our lives. Our unwillingness to release resentment against parents, our preference for expressing jealousy toward siblings, or our feelings of unworthiness are factors that act as a resistance to the easy flow of abundance into our lives.

There are no surprises in life. We are all open books. We can read our own book, or we can listen while others read it to us. Whenever we are ready, we can learn who we are and what we are up to. It just means paying attention—waking up.

Finally, we must be patient. Life unfolds at a perfect pace. Staying focused in the present moment offers us the perfect opportunity to address the precise issue that our inner knowing wishes us to focus on. Our inner knowing is an integral part of us. Becoming sensitive to its guidance brings us the benefit of the smartest part of our being.

When we set our own agenda, we reject a wonderful gift that our knowing part is offering to us. We are smarter than we think, and life is simpler than we believe. It is time for us to recognize this, appreciate it, and use it to open ourselves to the infinite abundance that is in us, and that is all around us.

As I mentioned previously, I conduct workshops without any notes. This allows me the benefit of much intuitive expression. One evening while leading a workshop, I startled myself as a new and surprising idea came forth. When something like that occurs, I assume that what I am saying is accurate and proceed as though it is. The concept I expressed was the definition of emotion. It withstood the attack of a psychotherapist that first night and has been quietly accepted by all participants ever since. I realize that the psychotherapist was, at least in part, voicing my own doubts about the definition. When he became convinced of the validity of the concept, so did I. Since it is, no longer necessary for me to question the definition, I do not attract participants who take issue with it.

15
Emotion

Emotion is a most interesting concept, and understanding it broadens our understanding of the other principles. Emotion is defined as *the attachment of a thought to a feeling.* Emotion is a concept that relates to energy. Thoughts and feelings are forms of energy. When we are at peace, we allow thoughts to flow freely through our minds and feelings to flow freely through our bodies. Anything that impedes the free flow of either one creates an energy block that we feel as discomfort.

How do we attach a thought to a feeling? By labeling, describing, defining, interpreting, or judging the feeling. The truth is that we are defining or interpreting something that we really know little about. Feelings aren't subject to understanding. They just are. They are like colors on an artist's canvas. One color isn't more beautiful, more meaningful, or better than another. Colors just are. When they occur together, each color provides a contrast for the others.

So it is with feelings. One is no better or more important than another. When, however, we intrude on their free flow by assigning them values and judging them, we create an energy block.

Consider the example of a friend who has just lost his job. He is on his way home and stops at your house to receive support for this unexpected event to which he is now responding and adjusting. Eager to express his feelings, he starts describing them to you. He uses

71

words like "upset," "anxious," and "concerned." He is interpreting the feelings he is experiencing. As he does this, he is literally stopping the feelings from flowing through his body. This creates an energy block that heightens his discomfort.

Let's assume that after fifteen minutes the phone rings. It is your friend's wife. She has just received a call from his employer. She reports that unexpectedly the company was given a very large contract and the employer has rehired your friend, offering him an increase in pay. Needless to say, the feelings that your friend now experiences are quite different. The words used to describe them would be, more likely, "relieved," "relaxed," "happy," or "elated."

Descriptions, evaluations, and interpretations of feelings, whether they are of a positive or negative nature, have the same effect. They stop the flow of feelings through the body.

There is no limit to the range of feelings that we can experience. Part of the beauty of life is to enjoy all the feelings we have. The varied circumstances of our lives give us the opportunity to experience many different kinds of feelings.

Looked at another way, feelings are energy vibrations. We can become sensitive to all of the various shades of vibrations and the various intensities of them. The only impediment to the full enjoyment of each and every vibration is the thinking process. Free of any interpretation, description, or evaluation, the vibration of every feeling is enjoyable. When we intervene in the process with our conscious minds, we create an energy block in our bodies.

The availability of sophisticated equipment has enabled scientists to shed light on this matter. When scientists wire subjects to instruments that monitor heartbeat, pulse, respiration, body temperature, and other physiological responses, and then induce so-called emotional reactions in the subjects, the scientists find that totally opposite emotional states produce similar physiological responses.

This helps us to understand how inaccurate our interpretation of our feelings really is. We generally give a feeling its meaning based on the context in which it occurs. When we are at a funeral service, we describe our feelings as sad. At a wedding or birthday party, we describe our feelings as happy. When preparing to take an important examination, we describe our feelings as anxious.

Our interpretation of our feelings is totally subjective and, as demonstrated by the scientists, bears no consistent relationship to the physiological changes in our bodies. In short, we make it up as we go along.

Anytime we interpret an experience as less than perfect the way it is, we create an illusion. By treating our evaluation of it as real, we keep that particular interpretation of the event alive. When we release the description or interpretation of it, and allow the feeling to flow freely through us, we encourage the true state of our being to come forth.

What, then, is the true state of our being? It is joyfulness. This is our natural state. Experiencing life in the context of joyfulness puts everything in its true perspective and brings us into alignment with our real selves and with the Universe.

And so, having gone full circle, we come back to the concept of perfection. If we allow ourselves to believe in it, and all that flows from it, we then open ourselves to the constant experience of our natural state, which is joyfulness. This is the way that we express our perfection and thus our gratitude for the incredible gifts that are given to us.

Question: Do you mean to say that feeling depressed or sad is not appropriate under any circumstances?

Answer: First a word about feelings. Whatever you are feeling, it is important to allow yourself to feel it fully. However, your characterization of your feelings as sad and depressed keeps you from feeling them. As long as you characterize or interpret your feelings, you are not feeling your feelings. You are feeling a distortion of them created by your interpretation of them.

When you are able to feel your feelings free of any characterization or interpretation, you are truly in touch with your feelings. Since our power resides in our feelings, feeling our feelings fully and freely gives us access to our power. The Feeling Exercise (chapter 29) is a three-step process that helps you reach this result.

73

Now back to the question. If, for example, someone close to you contracts an illness such as cancer or AIDS, a feeling other than peaceful seems appropriate. However, principle tells us that there are no accidents, and that nothing bad has happened. In fact, at the deepest levels this person has chosen this experience.

A question you can then ask yourself is "How can I best support my friend or relative under the circumstances?" One answer is by realizing that the disease process is not terrible and is reversible if the friend or relative chooses. The choice for healing requires a belief in the inherent power of the self to heal together with the desire to heal. Then what is healing? It is making peace with the internal conflict that is giving rise to the disease process.

A disease process often indicates an unwillingness of the ill person to be aware of the conflict, which is essentially an unwillingness to love himself under the specific circumstances of his present life.

For example, your friend or relative may still be angry at his parents for the way he was raised. He may prefer to retain the anger than release his judgment of them as inadequate or bad parents. As long as he maintains this position, which is his choice, he not only withholds love from his parents, but he also withholds love from himself. It is the lack of love of self that allows the disease process to take hold and then to advance.

When, in the presence of another, you feel the peace inside that comes from knowing that nothing terrible is happening and that only love is real, you inspire the other person to connect with this peace, which is his inner strength.

This is called empowerment, which may lead the ill person to choose to release his anger and resentment and ultimately feel love for his parents. If this choice is made, it means that your friend or relative has finally chosen to feel love for himself.

Question: If the only real feeling we have to express is joyfulness, how do you view funerals?

Answer: This is a great question and one that I am eager to answer. The truth is, no one ever dies. Funerals are a game we play in our society that represents a series of misperceptions of what life is all about. The basic misperception, aside from the fact that our essence, the real self, never dies, is that a person is not entitled to decide when to leave his physical body.

Infinite Intelligence granted free will for all. What right do any of us have to tell another person what to do or what not to do? Where do we draw the line? Will you allow me to tell you what color shirt, tie, or suit to wear, what to eat for dinner, what car to drive, what house or apartment to live in? Why should the spouse, children, and friends of a deceased person limit his right to leave his physical body at a particular time? How is that different from limiting his behavior in any other way? Doing so is an infringement on personal freedom.

Society creates the sadness around funerals. Since no one ever dies, in the real sense, and since we can, if we wish, maintain contact with people who have left their bodies, why all the trauma? When a person leaves on a cruise, we throw a party. A funeral can be like that—celebrating a trip that is more wonderful and certainly more interesting than a cruise.

Question: How do you suggest that I deal with a feeling such as anger? For example, I just learned that a person I had sexual relations with has AIDS. He didn't tell me, even though he knew that he was infected. I am very angry with him and the anger feels very real to me.

75

Answer: We both understand that you are having intense feelings when you think about the circumstances you have just related. What will finding fault with your sexual partner do to help you? Nothing. Expressing anger at him won't help you or him.

If you are angry, it means that you want to judge someone or something. As long as you wish to feel intense anger, you will create very intense situations, as you have done, to support you in feeling the intensity of anger you desire.

Until you are able to recognize that something akin to this is going on, you will continue to be angry—that is, you will continue to find fault with another, and you will feel the pain that goes with this intense amount of anger.

Releasing anger is a choice. The willingness to stop finding fault with another, or with oneself, is a choice. When we reach the place of willingness to release anger, and to stop finding fault with another or with ourselves, we can then allow the intense feelings we have to move freely through us. With this freedom of movement comes a feeling of relief, which settles into a feeling of peacefulness.

From this base of peacefulness we can open our hearts and allow the love energy within us to energize us.

In reality, all of us are all heart. Love is the only energy in the Universe. All pain is a result of withholding love from ourselves and others. Love is also the only healing force in the Universe. It is capable of healing AIDS and all other so-called disease processes.

When we find the love for ourselves and for others, we are ready to begin the healing process. The healing process is continued by locating, one at a time, each and every person and circumstance that we are angry at or are finding fault with. We must bring ourselves, through continuous practice, to a state of feeling forgiveness and eventually feeling love for each of these people.

While we are learning to heal ourselves by opening to the love within, it is important to use whatever other resources we are presently using, such as doctors and medicine. It is very self-supportive to avail ourselves of all kinds of support without judging any of them. If a particular method feels appropriate, use it. Love is compatible with everything. The more you feel love, the more benefit you will receive from whatever other method you are using.

The next topic addresses a subject that each of us is involved with almost continually—personal relationships. Improving the quality of our relationships certainly improves the quality of our lives.

16
Harmony in Relationships

Having a life that works perfectly requires harmony in relationships. In order to determine what harmony is, we look to the Universe for guidance. There we always find the perfect model. Since the Universe is a mutual support system, the key to harmonious relationships is the willingness to support others in the relationship and to allow them to support us. How is this best done? By seeing both them and ourselves as perfect just the way we are.

Anything less than perfection isn't real. It is an illusion. Seeing anger, confusion, anxiety, or fear in another person is just giving validity to an illusion. It also encourages the other person to believe that the illusion she is presenting is real. We can, if we are willing, disregard the illusion that the other person is expressing and see that person as the perfect, joyful person that she really is.

The more we practice, the easier it becomes. A simple way to practice is to glance at each stranger as she walks toward us on the sidewalk. Notice her facial expression and then immediately go behind it and see her as perfect and joyful. As we improve our ability to do this, we receive a marvelous benefit. We increase our ability to see ourselves as perfect and joyful.

Let's return to the concept of energy: Each of us emits energy signals all the time. Everything that happens to us is just something that we have asked for, something that we have signaled others to give us. To help you keep this concept in mind, remember my suggestion to think of yourself as totally surrounded by mirrors (see chapter 10). When what we see and feel creates discomfort, it is the Universe's way of reminding us that our perception is out of alignment. It is a signal to let go of whatever illusion we are involved in and to remind ourselves of our own and everyone else's perfection. When we see only beauty and love, it means that we are feeling only beauty and love.

When we are willing to see the other person as perfect just the way she is, the relationship becomes the best it can be for us. If it is appropriate for the relationship to continue, it will. If it is not, the relationship will draw to a close, peacefully.

People Present Themselves to Us the Way We Want Them To

As with the concept of abundance, the way we perceive harmony in relationships is the way we experience it. Becoming comfortable with the idea that people present themselves to us the way we want them to is a big step toward experiencing harmony in relationships. Remember, wanting something on a conscious level is not the only way to want it. Most of our wants are expressed on a subconscious level.

When we attract a person who acts less than lovingly toward us, that person is showing us a part of ourselves that we do not love and accept. The Universe, in Its infinite wisdom, is giving us the opportunity to see a part of us that we are hiding from ourselves. It is by recognizing this part of ourselves and loving it just the way it is that we release the energy locked in our bodies. It is then that the discomfort that we previously experienced disappears.

It is important to realize that *others cannot support us more than we support ourselves.* Achieving harmony in our relationships requires that we first be in harmony with ourselves. Focusing on the word "harmony" reminds us of our perfection and everyone else's. It brings us closer to experiencing harmony in relationships.

17
The Past and Forgiveness

One subject that attracts great attention is our past. And we seem particularly interested in how to release those parts of our past that seem to haunt us. Actually, any part of our past that influences us in the present is part of our present. And since only the present really exists, we can only release our present in the present.

Any discomfort that we experience is a result of locking energy in our bodies. More particularly, it is a result of attaching thoughts to feelings (see chapter 15). This means that we have judged something that has occurred, and the feelings that have been aroused are blocked in our bodies by the judgmental thoughts we have attached to them. We usually make this kind of interpretation when we perceive that another person is expressing less than unconditional love and support for us.

How, then, do we release the energy block? Stated another way, how do we detach the thought or judgment from the feeling? From my examination of the various alternatives offered, I find the simplest and most effective method to be the practice of forgiveness, which is really the complete suspension of judgment.

As we practice feeling forgiveness for the person whom we previously judged, or are now judging, as unloving toward us, we loosen the attachment of the judgment to the feeling. Since some of our judgments run deep and strong, we must practice feeling forgiveness for an extended period in order to release the judgment totally.

The Universe is continuously helping us to clear these blocks. It keeps sending us those people whom we need to forgive. Any time we are in the presence of someone whose behavior causes us discomfort, we know that that person represents someone, or is himself someone, whom we haven't forgiven. By forgiving the person in our present experience, we are also forgiving whomever that person might represent, even though we are unaware of any connection.

To take the matter full circle, the person each of us is actually forgiving is himself. Originally, someone made a judgment about our behavior. For example, a parent scolded us for being late for meals. At some point we adopted the belief about ourselves that when we are late for meals, we have done something wrong. Thereafter, any time we are angry because someone else is late for meals, a part of us still wants to come late for meals while another part believes that coming late for meals is inappropriate behavior.

When we are able to feel comfortable when someone else is late for meals, we know we have forgiven ourselves for coming late for meals. It also means that we have forgiven our actual parent, and the parent in us, who judged us for coming late for meals. Releasing the judgment of another is really releasing the judgment about ourselves. When we feel comfortable in the presence of another, we are really feeling comfortable with ourselves.

Forgiveness is another way of changing our perception of people and events. Judging anything is misperceiving it. Everything that occurs is just another event or experience. It is neither good nor bad, important nor unimportant, right nor wrong.

Why not allow ourselves to see perfection in every experience? Life is just a series of events that we attract in order to see a reflection of the state of our consciousness. Forgiveness releases any energy block and returns us to the joy that is our birthright.

Question: What happens when one person in a close relation-ship changes—how does it affect the relationship?

Answer: When one person in a relationship becomes more considerate, the other person responds. This is a result of the operation of several of the basic principles. Let's look at a few of them.

The law of cause and effect tells us that when a person truly wants a higher quality of life, he gets it. Such a person will be more forgiving, and those in his environment will pick up his expanded energy and respond to it in kind.

Consider the situation from the aspect of the principle that there is no right and no wrong. The person who stops finding fault with another person will certainly cause the other person to respond differently in the relationship.

Following another principle will lead to an even more dramatic improvement in a relationship. Consider the effect of consistently seeing another person as perfect just the way he is.

In summary, then, any time one person in a previously troubled relationship moves into alignment with universal principles, the love that was previously withheld is now allowed to flow between the parties. Since the past always merges with the present, the new loving relationship erases, through transformation, the prior unloving relationship. A forgiving attitude, with its ability to open hearts, is one of the most loving gifts we can ever give to ourselves.

I'm going to take a break now and go for a walk.

18
Unity

To understand the concept of perfection, it is necessary to understand the relationship each of us has to the Universe, which is our Source, and the relationship we have to each other. Underneath all of our apparent differences, the essence of each of us is not only perfect but in many ways the same. This is inherent in the concept of perfection.

As mentioned in other chapters, we can continually look behind the projection of other people's attitudes, expressions, and emotions, and notice only their perfection. This also helps us to remember that the Universe is an experience of wholeness—a unity of all of its parts.

We believe in our own perfection only when we believe that everyone else is also perfect. When we see another person as less than perfect, we really see and feel our own imperfection. This happens so that we are made aware of that part of ourselves that we do not love. We should be grateful for these experiences. When we learn to love another person, we are really learning to love a part of ourselves that we previously rejected.

A simple way to do this is to first locate a quiet and peaceful time and place. Bring into your mind the person whom you see as less than perfect. Then see yourself feeling comfortable in the presence of that person. When you have pleasurable feelings about that person, you have learned to love a part of yourself that you previously did not love.

Sometimes you may find it difficult to generate pleasant feelings about someone. If this is the case, there is an intermediate step that is very useful—feeling forgiveness (see chapter 17). This is the bridge between our present feelings of discomfort about a person and our learning to love her unconditionally. When practicing forgiveness, it is important first to feel forgiveness for the other person for all the things she did or does that we perceive as less than loving. We must, however, also feel forgiveness for ourselves for all the things that we have done that we believe are less than loving with respect to that person.

If we are going to be successful in achieving the feeling of forgiveness for another and for ourselves, it is important that we release time as a factor—that is, not set limits on how long the process should take or when it should happen. Our focus must be on our intention to finally forgive, and we must be willing to persevere in practicing forgiveness until we succeed.

It is also important for us to remain aware of each time we do not feel forgiving. This is a signal to strengthen our resolve to practice feeling forgiveness for that particular person and for ourselves. Everyone is always entitled to forgiveness. Since each of us is, in essence, a part of everyone else, we cannot achieve total forgiveness for ourselves until we have totally forgiven everyone else. Our progress in seeing another's perfection is also our progress in seeing the Universe as a unified whole—a unity of perfect parts.

Question: When I think of all the people I now interact with, from my boss to certain relatives and friends, I realize how much other people's behavior bothers me. It seems like an overwhelming task to forgive all these people, see them as perfect just the way they are, and learn to love them. How can I achieve this state?

Answer: How successful you will be, and in fact whether it will be an impossible task or an interesting challenge, is up to you. In order to win the game of life, we have to keep asking ourselves, "What is the real game?" If we conclude that the real game is having money, assets, a better house and car, more vacations, and more status and power in our community, then forgiving anyone is virtually impossible. If we see as our purpose in life the mastery of the universal truths that support it, and consider that to be the real game, then learning to forgive others and finally loving them can actually be fun.

Infinite Intelligence is our silent Partner as we go through life. Whenever we choose to play the real game, we notice that our Partner provides us with incredible support. In fact, just the decision to play the real game guarantees that we cannot lose. Playing this game also leads us to conclude that each of us is a perfect part of a perfect wholeness and that we have come together to know and feel our unity.

19
Time

The concept of time helps us to understand how the other concepts relate to each other. Society teaches us that time occurs in three stages: the past, the present, and the future. In fact, there is only one time that is real—the present. The past is gone; it no longer exists. The future is yet to occur. Only the present moment ever really exists. What we believe creates our experience at that moment. When we expand our beliefs about anything, the old beliefs are gone. We function according to the new belief, since we can have only one operative belief about anything at any one time.

Our concept of time influences our perception of our experiences. We tend to see present experiences in the light of past experiences—in other words, we expect things to remain pretty much the same as they have always been. This is especially true of the way we respond to people. We draw conclusions about the people we interact with, and the next time we are with them we expect them to behave in accordance with our preconceived beliefs about them.

Consider the following example: You are walking down the street and meet a friend who introduces you to the person he is with. This person is obviously impatient and pays little attention to you after he is introduced. While you talk to your friend for a few minutes, the other person waits politely but is obviously growing more impatient and is eager to leave. You next meet this person at a party. As soon as you see him, you remember how impatient he was. This intrudes on your readiness to find out what he is really like.

You were not aware that when you first met this person, he had just come from visiting his mother, who was critically ill. He was eager to discuss certain decisions about his mother's treatment with his friend. Without realizing it, you were delaying that discussion.

Having drawn certain conclusions about a person, we thereafter expect him to act in accordance with these conclusions. Our expectation about how he will act encourages him to act that way. Seeing the present through the eyes of the past distorts our view of the present. Consciously or subconsciously remembering how a person behaved previously hampers our ability to relate to the perfection of that person in the present.

That's like comparing last night's sunset with the one we are now seeing. Each sunset is different from the ones before it. Comparing the one we are looking at with past sunsets detracts from our ability to fully experience the one we are viewing. Describing it in any way also limits our ability to experience it fully, for in describing it, we move our focus away from all our sensory organs, which are responding to its beauty, and concentrate on our intellect. When we lead with our minds, we tend to bypass our hearts. And it is through our hearts that we feel and enjoy the beauty of life.

Let's look at another hypothetical situation: You are in your home with a group of friends. The phone rings, and the caller tells you that a man is on his way to see you. He is a very special man, a hero, who has just saved many people in a burning building, at great risk to his own life. You hang up and tell your friends about the call and about the man who is on his way. Everyone is excited and can't wait to meet him.

When the doorbell rings, you welcome the hero and express your appreciation for his wonderful accomplishment. After several minutes, the phone rings again. It is the same caller. She apologizes for the previous call and tells you that there has been a terrible mistake. The man who is in your living room isn't a hero. He is a murderer. Instead of saving many people, he has just killed them. Needless to say, your reaction and that of all the others in the room toward the visitor changes instantly, as you are all in fear of your lives.

Perhaps the man just wandered in from the street and is neither a hero nor a killer.

This story illustrates how what you believe at any time creates a reality for you. When we see only perfection in someone, what we are told about him does not influence us one way or another. That person is then free to respond to us in a way that is consistent with the way we see and feel about him.

Learning to be totally in the present, the only time that ever exists, is a skill that requires constant practice. We learn to remind ourselves continually that whatever we are presently experiencing is unique. It has never happened before. It will never happen again. We are free to see the present differently from the way we ever saw it before.

However, perfection cannot be experienced as a thought. It can only be felt. How do we feel another person's perfection? By opening our hearts to that person. Our hearts feel only perfection. That is their primary function. When we open our hearts, we can also use them to see with. When we wish to see and feel the truth about ourselves and about others, all we need to do is to open our hearts and relate heart to heart. Our hearts are our most valuable asset. They are our source of truth, wisdom, peace, and joy. There is nothing we cannot heal with an open heart.

Question: Much of our lives revolve around the clock. We concern ourselves with getting to work on time, completing jobs on time, and meeting people on time. How do you suggest we learn the new concept of time?

Answer: The solution to any problem is always the same. Look for a universal principle and view it from that perspective. Stated another way, to solve a problem that you are experiencing at the level of illusion, go to a higher level of thought.

Whenever time appears to be a problem for us, one concept we can introduce is the law of cause and effect. We can remind ourselves that we have created a situation where time apperars to be an issue. After we have released any judgment of ourselves or anyone

91

else for having created the situation, we can then see how time is not the issue.

Let's make it specific: Assume that your boss wants you to finish a report by a certain date. You think that he hasn't given you enough time. We both know that when one truly wants to do something, ideas flow rapidly and easily. For whatever reason, if you feel you can't finish the report on time, you really don't want to finish it on time.

Shifting your focus to universal principles allows you to locate the real issue—the fact that you are withholding love from your boss.

To continue with the example, allow yourself to examine your thoughts about your boss, your job, and the particular assignment. If any of your thoughts are judgmental, you can practice releasing your judgments of your boss and, when you are ready, move to a place of feeling love for him. You will then be relating to him heart to heart. Not only will your relationship with your boss become comfortable, you will have released the illusion that time is a problem.

We can understand from the foregoing illustration that mastery of the principles requires great perseverance. We must be relentless. The principles are in effect all the time, whether we pay attention to them or not. They are available for our use all the time. However, they work for us only when we use them. When we disregard them, the discomfort we feel is a signal from the Universe to view the situation in terms of principle. The choice is always ours.

20
What We Focus
On Expands

Our beliefs attract additional thoughts that are consistent with those beliefs. For example, let's say you are scheduled for a job interview as an executive secretary. You are concerned about the interview. The following thoughts cross your mind: "I will appear nervous. I will not type as well as I can because of the pressure of being judged. Other applicants will have more skills or present themselves better at their interviews."

Since our existing beliefs continually attract thoughts that are consistent with those beliefs, our lives continue to expand in the direction of our existing beliefs. In the example just cited, aren't you more likely to appear nervous because of your negative thoughts about yourself?

If we wish to improve the quality of our lives, we must expand our beliefs. Let's go back to the example. Suppose that you talk with a friend who reminds you of your many and varied office skills. Your friend also tells you that you are highly qualified for the job and that the prospective employer should be eager to hire you. You think about your skills and realize that your friend is correct. This leads to thoughts such as "It will be fun to work for the new company. This position will give me the opportunity to use my creative writing talent." You are now feeling confident about the situation, which will lead to a favorable interview.

The quality of our life is related directly to the objective we seek. When we keep our focus on our universal purpose and on universal principles, we ensure that the quality of our life will be the best that it can be.

To implement the concept of *what we focus on expands*, we must realize that, at times, although we believe we are focusing on one thing, we are really focusing on something else. For example, let us assume that you are very distressed because you owe a great deal of money and can't see how you can pay all your bills. You decide to place your focus on having lots of money. You repeat to yourself, over and over, "I am rich, I am rich." But you still feel distressed. Since you don't really believe the statements you are repeating, they just serve to arouse your existing fear of not being able to pay your bills. While you are saying "I am rich, I am rich" you are feeling "I am poor, I am poor." Thus your focus is really on the latter. In fact, making these statements heightens your distress because you are, in effect, focusing on your distress, which is your fear of not being able to pay your bills.

Until you are able to release your fear, you will continue to feel the distress and to attract circumstances that are consistent with your fear—namely, more bills than income.

It is important to become aware of what we really believe, if we wish to improve the result we are receiving. In this case, principle tells us that fear is a withholding of love. Until we locate whom we really wish to withhold love from, forgive that person, and then feel love for her, we shall continue to experience a shortage of funds to repay the debt. When we finally feel love for the person, we shall either create the necessary abundance to give generously to her or receive her forgiveness of the debt. It is that simple.

Question: You say that we should not focus on material wealth. If we don't focus on it, how can we achieve it?

Answer: The principle involved is that the Universe is a place of abundance. For us to be experiencing less than total abundance means that we are literally pushing it away from ourselves. Abundance naturally wants to flow through our lives. That is why we do not have to attempt to bring it in. The process is one of releasing beliefs and patterns that block the flow of abundance. If we just do what we love, love what we do, and express ourselves fully and freely, we are serving others in accordance with our purpose. All that is left is for us to open ourselves to receive.

Since this is such an important principle, let me state it another way. As long as we believe that in order to have money we must work for it, we guarantee that we shall have to work to obtain money. Until we can feel the abundance of the Universe, we have to keep reminding ourselves that this is our natural state. We cannot remind ourselves too often. When the shift in our belief occurs, then the shift occurs in the flow of dollars and other forms of abundance into our lives.

There is another factor that is significant in opening ourselves to our natural state of abundance. Very often we hold abundance hostage by our unwillingness to make peace with parents and other significant people in our lives. The key to abundance is in our heart. When we close our heart to anyone, particularly someone who is deeply connected to us, as a parent is, we lock the door to our abundance.

Making peace with our parents often requires great perseverance and always requires 100 percent intention. Be patient with yourself. Consistency is a most valuable quality. Be satisfied with small gains, steadily made. Open yourself a little at a time to the love that is in you for your parents and for everyone, including yourself.

When you feel deep love for your parents and for yourself, you will know what abundance is all about. Material abundance flows from love. It is a derivative of love. And love is deeper and more powerful than words can express. You will understand it when you allow yourself to experience it.

95

21
Trust

We always experience what we believe. In order to have the benefit of the concept of perfection, we must first believe it, trust it. Our belief in the perfection of Infinite Intelligence allows us to relinquish use of our conscious, rational mind and to defer to our intuition.

Learning to believe in perfection is really a process of release. It is letting go of the belief that we and the Universe are less than perfect just the way we are. The more we believe in perfection, the more we are willing to let go of thoughts that are in opposition to it. We are then able to trust the Universe to give us the benefits of Its perfection.

We demonstrate our trust in perfection when we surrender the use of our conscious minds to our intuition; when we express our talents fully and freely; when we allow ourselves to be inspired and to inspire others; when we keep reaching for more enlivening experiences; and when we see beyond the way people outwardly express themselves and, instead, see and feel them with our hearts.

As we increase our belief in the perfection of the Universe, and all that this implies, we increase our willingness to trust that we are living our lives in a way that works perfectly.

Question: I understand what you are saying on an intellectual level, but when I think of leaving my present job for a more perfect one and trusting that the natural abun-

Answer:

dance of the Universe is there for my support, I notice I don't really feel trusting. How can I bridge the gap? This is a situation faced by many people who are trying to improve the quality of their lives. The process of integrating universal principles into our lives continually brings us up to our personal boundary, our point of resistance to accepting one or more of the universal principles. In the interest of simplifying the process, it is helpful to see it as a game and then to enjoy the pleasure of playing the game.

One of the techniques that we have to master to play this game successfully is learning to trust. The only way we can truly learn a principle is to experience it. We have to test ourselves. That requires trust, which is an inherent part of the real game of life. We must keep asking ourselves, "What is real and what is illusion in our lives?" We will not give up an illusion if we do not believe that the Universe truly supports us. It is only when we trust that we allow support into our lives.

The next step is always the same. We must notice the gap between what we believe and what we would like to believe. What do we really believe about the principles? It doesn't serve us to make changes before we are ready. By reminding ourselves, as often as necessary, of the gap between what we really believe and what we would like to believe, we keep narrowing that gap, so that one morning we'll wake up and realize that we really do trust that the Universe is on our side and that it does support us to the full extent that we are open to receive Its unlimited abundance.

There is another aspect of your question that requires a response. In order to find a more perfect job, it is important to remember that your present job is not an accident or a mistake. Wherever you are is purposeful. You are there because the deepest and most knowing part of you placed you there. Until you are at peace with this, which means being at peace with all

98

the people and all the circumstances of your present job, moving on to another job will be an exercise in futility, for you will take with you to your next job the same conflicts and discomfort you feel at your present job.

The important fact to recognize is that discomfort and dissatisfaction is within *us*, not in another person or in the circumstances—in this case, the conditions of your present job. The things you are judging in your present job as less than perfect are the very things you must make peace with so that you can go peacefully to your next position.

It is not until we learn to love ourselves just the way we are that we begin to allow our lives to become truly satisfying and fulfilling. And we will not love ourselves the way we are until we are also willing to love others the way they are.

The talents we have are a source of great joy and fulfillment. We give ourselves the generous gift of expressing them when we first feel good enough about ourselves to believe that we deserve such an extraordinary gift.

There is also another part to the gift. After we feel good enough about ourselves to allow ourselves the joy of doing what we love, we must then increase our love for ourselves to the point where we permit ourselves to experience significant abundance while doing what we love.

Learning to trust the Universe is really an aspect of trusting ourselves. And trust for the Universe derives from loving the Universe and feeling Its love. This also means loving ourselves. For, in truth, we and the Universe are ONE.

22
Comfort and Discomfort

The Universe sends us two basic signals as indicators of our degree of alignment with It. Comfort is evidence of our being in alignment; discomfort is evidence of our being out of alignment. Our degree of comfort or discomfort is in proportion to the degree of our alignment or misalignment with the Universe. The signals in our bodies can range from excruciating pain to bliss.

What makes this principle most interesting is that we are always dealing only with our perception. Thus, *it is our interpretation of a situation, rather than anything inherent in that situation, that determines whether it will be a source of comfort or discomfort to us.*

To understand the concept of comfort and discomfort, we must first expand our concept of ourselves. We are not only our bodies, thoughts, feelings, beliefs, experiences, or any of the things we own or use. We are primarily our essence, which is God substance, and so is everyone and everything else. This means that we are not separate from anyone or anything. Our discomfort arises from our perception that we are separate from other people and things, and from God, and that we are limited to our bodies, thoughts, and feelings.

Our life in the human experience is an opportunity to transcend this limited perception. We do this by learning to make peace with

101

everything just the way it is, which is also accepting everything as perfect just the way it is.

Extending this concept that we are primarily our essence can help us to understand the world of illusion. Whatever thoughts, beliefs, or agreements are current in the world at any time are perfect just the way they are. These thoughts, beliefs, and agreements do influence how people act and the results they achieve, but they do not alter the underlying perfection that is the essence of each person and the inherent state of the Universe.

To use the signals of comfort and discomfort correctly, we have to interpret them differently from the way we were taught. Society encourages us to believe that withstanding discomfort is essential to advancement in areas such as career, marriage, raising children, and building a secure future. To offset this misperception, we must continually remind ourselves to view these signals in the way we intuitively want to read them. It takes a lot of practice to allow our lives to be comfortable, easy, and fun.

A word of caution: When you decide to learn to accept everything as perfect just the way it is, it is prudent to provide yourself with as supportive an environment as possible—preferably a support group of one or more people who will give you unconditional love and support during this process (see chapter 42).

Remember, the Universe is a mutual support system, and each of us has a deep inner need to function in a mutually supportive environment. Providing ourselves with this environment is the path to a successful transition and ultimately to a life of total joy.

Question: I can think of many ways I can experience comfort in my body. I can take a drink, eat some chocolate cake, smoke, or watch a ball game. You seem to be talking about something else. What do you mean?

Answer: The signals of comfort and discomfort that I am talking about are on a deeper level than the examples you gave. I am referring to feeling comfort or discomfort as we face the situations that life presents to us.

The knowing part of us is always available to guide us. The knowing part is in our heart and connects with

102

other hearts. Using our heart to guide us ensures the best possible result. In simplest terms, when our heart is closed, we feel discomfort, and when our heart is open, we feel comfort.

23
The Sponge

Our consciousness is like a sponge. We can fill it with our own intuitive ideas and decisions. We can fill it with clear intentions to make peace with everything just the way it is. Or, if we leave the sponge partly dry, the world around us gladly fills it for us.

In our society there are powerful influences focused on each of us all the time—television, radio, newspapers, magazines, salesmen, employers, relatives, and friends. They have many ideas about what we should be thinking and doing. When we avoid making clear choices about the quality of life we wish, we tend to adopt the ideas from these other sources, often without being aware that we are doing so.

The solution is simple. We can start each day with a clear intention to feel peaceful all day. We can do the Feeling Exercise (see chapter 29) regularly. We can keep the quality of life we wish for ourselves uppermost in our consciousness. The choice is always ours. When we avoid making this choice, others make the choice for us.

Fill your own sponge with the intention to see the perfection in everything just the way it is and to feel peacefulness above all else.

Question: How does the suggestion to fill our own sponge align with the principle that the Universe handles the details?

Answer: If you examine the suggestion I made as to how to fill the sponge, you will see that I suggest focusing on the *quality* of our life, not on its details. Our role is to focus on feeling peaceful and to allow the Universe to send us those people and events that will support us in achieving a life of peace and fulfillment.

24
Negative Thoughts and Judgments

What is a negative thought? It is any thought that does not recognize the perfection of the Universe and everything in it. This definition classifies any thought that expresses a judgment as negative. When we judge anything or anyone, we confirm an illusion.

Consider the following example: You are viewing a painting, and a person standing next to you asks you for an opinion of the painting. If your answer is based on your reaction to the shapes and colors on the canvas, you are missing the point—the painting provides a creative interaction between you and the artist. It is the artist's desire to reveal and express herself to you—that is the purpose of her creation. When you receive that communication, when you open your heart to it, you are best supporting the artist and yourself. You are also enjoying the perfection of the experience.

Brought to its logical conclusion, seeing and feeling the perfection of everyone and everything encourages others to express that perfection. If we judge the result, we limit rather than encourage free expression.

Remember, each of us is here to express our talents fully and freely. Whatever encourages us to express these talents supports us. This in turn supports the Universe. Making judgments limits full and free expression of talent.

·A comment for those who fear that if we do not judge the quality of a person's expression, society will not properly encourage the production of higher quality goods and services: When we do what we love, we are expressing those unique qualities and talents that the Universe has given us. Our performance, motivated by the joy it generates, automatically produces the highest quality of which we are capable. This is all part of the perfection of the universal plan (see chapter 5).

When We Cease Judging Others, We Are at Peace with Ourselves

Remember also, whenever we find fault with anyone, we are really judging the part of ourselves that wishes to act in the same way. Until we cease judging others, we are not at peace within ourselves. Stated another way, when we are at peace with everyone and everything, then we are at peace with ourselves. We make peace with others to create peace within ourselves.

Question: Please amplify the comments about not judging the work product of anyone. How is that truly supportive of the person?

Answer: This issue is one I remember discussing in college. It seems to be an issue that comes up often and has meaning for many of us. If one of the basic principles is that life is a mutual support system, then how do we best support another person? Do we help the person by pointing out that her performance is less than perfect, from our point of view?

We must recognize that we are our essences, which are perfect. We are not our work product, our thoughts, or our actions. By judging anything about a person, we support that person's belief that she is not perfect just the way she is. Whatever a person expresses is, at that moment, the closest that she is able to come to expressing her true essence, the perfect part of herself. We always have the choice of supporting either an illusion of or the real self of another person. The choice is up to each of us in every situation.

We do not encourage a person by telling her how she has failed, or how she has expressed herself imperfectly. Rather, we encourage a person by noticing all the ways in which she is already perfect.

Accepting everything as perfect just the way it is does not preclude our choosing freely from among the people, products, and services available to us. We can choose to listen to Bach rather than to Chopin, to play tennis rather than golf, to eat spaghetti rather than steak, or to choose one employee rather than another, without judging any of our choices as either good or bad.

I have a few observations about seeing the perfection in another and not judging the person even though her performance (product or service) is not satisfactory to us. The person whose product or service is not satisfactory will learn about it from the inevitable result—people will choose other products and services. If we judge a person, we encourage her to feel less worthy and less capable. This attitude tends to discourage her from looking within to become aware of the ways she is withholding love from herself. In fact, by having been judged, she will tend to love herself a lot less.

When a person loves herself, she automatically acts in ways that are self-supportive. Becoming self-supportive requires self-discipline. I define self-discipline as a choice a person makes to handle her life in a way that leads to a deep sense of fulfillment.

Discipline imposed by another, the form of discipline most of us have learned, is the opposite of self-discipline. Until self-discipline is learned and appreciated, a person cannot achieve true success and fulfillment. This means first forgiving all the people we are still angry at for teaching us discipline by the force of their will over ours.

Self-discipline is the greatest friend a person can have. It is the vehicle to successful results in any endeavor. It is an essential prerequisite to creative expression of a talent, for without self-discipline the expression is usually too random and scattered to be truly useful.

In summary, then, let me reiterate that judging anyone locks up the energy around the existing situation and discourages self-love, which precludes self-discipline and encourages a person to follow a path away from expressing her talent fully, freely, creatively, and abundantly.

You might want to take a break now.

25
Aliveness

Our bodies are finely tuned instruments that are designed to function perfectly as the energy of the Universe flows freely through them. When we allow this to happen, we experience the feeling of aliveness. Anything that impedes the free flow of energy through us reduces our feeling of aliveness. In the same way that releasing our judgment of a feeling opens us to our joyfulness, so does the releasing of any block in the free flow of our energy lead to a feeling of aliveness. The culprit that can impede the free flow of energy is the conscious mind. When we are able to trust that whatever is is perfect just the way it is, and are able to totally surrender to the perfection of the present moment, we shall know what aliveness is all about.

Being at peace with the perfection of what is just the way it is opens us to our inspiration. This is the part of us that wants to fly, to soar, to express our uniqueness in ways that enable us to feel the true joy and beauty of our real selves.

We are capable of being inspired all the time. Remember, perfection already exists. Our role is to recognize it and place ourselves in alignment with it, letting go of all beliefs that are in opposition to it.

We can always look for, notice, and acknowledge our own and everyone else's magnificence. It is always there. It's fun to be magnificent and to play with other magnificent people.

You can live your life any way you choose. Choose inspiration! Choose aliveness!

Question: You refer again to the conscious mind as the major impediment in our lives. Why, then, was it given to us?

Answer: The only way I can justify the existence of the conscious mind is that it gives validity to the universal principle of free will and free choice. For each of us to make choices, we require a mechanism. That mechanism is the conscious mind.

Our society believes that use of the conscious mind is essential to improve the quality of our lives. We are taught to evaluate, judge, analyze, and interpret everything. The willingness to substitute Infinite Intelligence, our inner knowing, for our conscious-mind intelligence, which society has grossly overrated, takes a lot of trust, faith, and perseverance. Yet without that expression of trust, faith, and perseverance, we forego the opportunity to bring fulfillment into our lives through the ultimate experiences of peacefulness, aliveness, inspiration, and joy.

26
Mastery

When have we achieved mastery of something? When we feel confident that the thing we are trying to master is working perfectly. We release any concern or thought about it, and let go of any need to influence or control it.

Take tennis as an example. The professionals who have mastered the game assume that they know how to hit the ball correctly and just go ahead and hit it. Most people have achieved mastery of their experience with food. They assume that their bodies will do what is necessary to digest the food they consume. The average person does not worry about whether his glands will secrete the proper enzymes or whether his blood will carry nutrients to the cells.

The same applies to our experience with money. We have mastered money when it is no longer a concern in our lives. We trust it to function perfectly. We go on with the rest of our lives doing what we love and allow the money to take care of itself.

It's important to realize that money is just a form of energy. If we wish it to flow freely in our lives, we must have no attachment to it and no concern about it. Thoughts of concern or attachment create energy blocks and impede the flow. Trusting the Universe to provide us with what is best for us at all times will ensure a free flow of money and everything else.

The Paradox of the Material World

Having a life of material abundance is simple, yet most people fail to achieve it. It is like trying to grasp a particle floating in the air. When we try too hard, it eludes our grasp. When we approach it slowly, gently, and lovingly, it cooperates and allows us to have it.

The key to being in a relaxed, comfortable state that allows us to approach life in a gentle, loving manner is the belief that material abundance is our gift from the Universe. We need do only one thing to have it—play the real game. Whenever we focus on the spiritual aspect of life, the material aspect comes along as a gift. Going after material wealth directly will always be a struggle, and the cost will always exceed the benefit gained.

Question: How can it all be so simple and easy?
Answer: The Universe is an experience of ease and simplicity. One of the ways that you know you are dealing with universal principles is that the concepts are simple and easy. This is inherent in the concept of perfection. The Universe is, by definition, simply perfect. When you notice that something is complicated, be suspicious. It is probably not in alignment with the Universe and Its principles.

The next discussion is of awareness, which is the state of being conscious. The opposite is being unconscious, a word we apply to someone who is not alert to what is really going on. It is important not only that we be alert, but that we reach for a state of heightened awareness. Let's start by taking a look at the concept of awareness.

27
Awareness

Most of us spend much of our time responding to descriptions of what is happening rather than to what is really happening. We believe that we can comprehend everything that happens, so we reduce every experience to something that we can describe. The description then becomes a substitute for the experience.

There is a simple way to find the meaning of life. Paradoxically, understanding comes only when we do not try to understand. It is unfolded to us as we allow ourselves to be aware of our experiences without evaluating, analyzing, or describing them.

Each of us has a built-in mechanism that is designed to guide us toward perfect responses to all events and experiences in our lives. I call this the Perfect Response Mechanism (PRM). It is the mechanism that is brilliant enough to digest food and take nutrients to the cells in order to support the life of the organism. It is the mechanism that enables a fielder to race to where a baseball will be hit, even before he can have any conscious-mind knowledge of where the ball is going. This mechanism can respond to an infinite number of stimuli instantaneously and simultaneously, if we allow the stimuli to reach the mechanism unimpeded. Every time the conscious mind intervenes in any way to evaluate, analyze, or think about the stimulus, the PRM cannot do its job perfectly. It is akin to having a calculator available and doing all of our calculations without using it.

To simplify the concept of the PRM, think of all of your sensory organs (eyes, ears, nose, skin, etc.) as located at one end of a tube. Visualize the PRM at the other end of the tube. Picture a hinged flap across the middle of the inside of the tube. The flap represents your conscious mind. Every time your conscious mind intervenes by evaluating, analyzing, describing, or judging any stimulus, the flap drops across the tube. This prevents the stimulus from passing through the tube to the PRM.

Whether we use it or not, the PRM is always available. When we use it, its brilliance is immediately evident. My suggestion is to use the PRM as often as possible. This requires us to keep our conscious minds from intervening.

Here are some simple exercises to help you to do this:

Think of the places where you generally spend your time. Then create an awareness exercise that focuses your conscious mind on something in the immediate environment. Choose something that is appropriate to the environment and is interesting enough to keep the conscious mind engaged. For example, when driving your car, notice the energy changes that take place each time another vehicle passes by. Notice the difference in energy between a car passing in your direction and one going in the opposite direction. Notice the difference in energy between passing a car or a large truck and passing parked cars or trees.

When in your house or apartment, select a dominant feature of each room to focus on whenever you enter the room. For example, focus on odors when you go into your kitchen, or colors when you are in your living room. Focus on the texture or taste of each food while you are eating. It's fun to make up these exercises. Change them as often as is necessary to keep your conscious mind interested. When you lose interest, the conscious mind becomes free to roam around, and it will often intervene between the stimuli and the PRM.

The beauty of these exercises is that the focus on one aspect of the immediate environment enhances the ability of the PRM to receive all other stimuli from that environment. The PRM not only responds perfectly to each stimulus, but its sequence of responses is also perfect.

Let's return to the example of the car. Focusing our conscious minds on the energy changes while we drive along prevents us from evaluating the experience. (This keeps the flap in the tube in its open position and allows all of the stimuli in our immediate environment to pass directly from our sensory organs to the PRM.) Stimuli such as road noises, fumes, and tensions in our bodies are received by the PRM. The perfect response or sequence of responses is then transmitted to us intuitively.

If we allow ourselves to evaluate the experience, we quickly find ourselves conceptualizing the situation. We think such thoughts as "What an annoying trip this is" or "This highway is like a big parking lot." Once we conceptualize or judge the experience, we inhibit the natural operation of our PRM.

Our PRM is constantly leading us in the direction of a higher quality of life. For example, when we heighten our awareness of the energy changes around our car, we notice these energies as sounds which, with more heightened awareness, become a symphony of sounds. This in turn heightens our awareness of the various odors around us which, through our ever greater sensitivity to them, become so delicate that we perceive them as a bouquet of aromas. We then notice that each day the symphony of sounds and the bouquet of aromas change. We find ourselves looking forward to driving.

We further find that heightening our awareness to the sounds and aromas as we drive causes us to heighten our awareness to them wherever we are. Sounds become symphonies when we walk down a street. Aromas become bouquets when we prepare the foods and then eat them for dinner.

This heightened awareness so improves the quality of our life that it may inspire us to, for example, create a support group at work. This support group turns an ordinary and somewhat pleasant work environment into one where each employee reaches out in support of another, and where everyone desires to feel more love for one another. What started out as just a group of people working in one place transforms into a closely knit team of people who, out of their love for each other, radiate love and support to the whole company and its customers.

PRM and Relationships

Person-to-person interaction presents us with the most challenging context in which to use the PRM, because each of us is very good at convincing others that the way we present ourselves is the way we really are. We express anger, come late for appointments, act confused, or show disrespect for the feelings of others.

Strange as it may seem, anger is just a distorted expression of love. It is the nearest a person can come to expressing love at that moment. When someone is able to see past the anger, and refuses to believe it, the angry person responds by releasing the anger.

So we come back once again to square one. Our experience of the world is determined by how we see it. When we practice seeing others as really loving us (in spite of how unloving their actions might be), we notice that our world changes to reflect our new perception of it.

The following awareness exercise illustrates how you can deal with an emotional illusion. Assume that you are experiencing what you perceive as anger toward another person.

Remind yourself that anger is an illusion, a distortion you have created. Let go of the description of the experience you are having and just focus on the sensation in your body. The key element is breaking the connection between the sensation in your body and any thoughts attached to it. Once you release all your thoughts about the sensation and focus only on the sensation itself, the sensation will disappear. What is left is the underlying feeling, which can now be enjoyed free of distortion.

Feel forgiveness for the other person. Then feel forgiveness for yourself.

> Focus your attention on anything that induces a state of comfort and peacefulness. Do something that you love to do.

The PRM is the active participant in the exercise. It always seeks to provide the perfect response to any situation and to bring you back to your natural state of comfort. By eliminating your evaluation of the situation, you allow the stimulus to go unimpeded to the PRM, which can then act appropriately.

If there is a strong connection between any of your thoughts and your feelings, it can take much repetition to break that connection. Continuing with the exercise will bring about changes in energy flow and in the nature of the sensations in your body. As the connection is weakened, energy is released. When the connection is finally broken, you will respond spontaneously and freely to the person who induced the discomfort in the first place.

Question: You stated that our PRM wants to lead us to a more peaceful experience. You also stated that for us to improve the quality of our lives, we must actively focus on doing so. There seems to be an inconsistency between the two thoughts. How can they be reconciled?

Answer: The PRM is the part of each of us that is connected to Infinite Intelligence. That is how it knows how to respond perfectly to every situation. If we had no preconceived ideas and beliefs as to how the world worked and, instead, just allowed the Universe to guide us, we would continually experience the beauty of life. What stands in the way are our beliefs and our vested interests, our wanting to have things a certain way. However, until these beliefs are expanded we must actively focus on the process of expanding them.

The awareness exercises suggested in this chapter and the exercises and suggestions made in other chapters, if practiced consistently, will help you reach those states of comfort and happiness that life is really all about. The more we can experience being there, the greater our incentive to open the energy around all beliefs that keep us from staying there.

119

28
Our Relationship with Our Source

Do you believe that God or an Infinite Intelligence is the creative force and the support for human life and everything else in the Universe? If your answer is yes, do you see God as an unconditionally loving and supportive energy? It is important to realize that the way you view this energy is exactly the way that you will experience life. If you can bring yourself to honestly believe that God is totally loving and supportive of everyone, under all circumstances, then you will experience a life of total joy. The extent to which your belief is less than that is the extent to which your life will be less than totally joyful.

There are people who believe that it is better to focus on a concept other than God to explain the creation of the Universe. When this is an attempt to avoid the concept of God, because thoughts related to God are unpleasant, then the replacement will not relieve the discomfort.

As long as we harbor any thoughts that God is less than a totally loving and supportive Entity, such thoughts will block us from achieving the peace of mind and joy that we wish to achieve.

When we view God as less than a totally loving and supportive Entity, we view people as less than totally loving and supportive. Those of us who can see the perfection and unconditional love of God can see the same quality in others and in the Universe.

In our relationship with our Universe and with other people, we are truly experiencing the mirror image of our beliefs. This is a very simple yet powerful concept. The best investment we can ever make is to learn to see everything and everyone around us as an expression of God, for then we see ourselves that way and we actually experience life that way.

God Is Our Friend

Viewed another way, God is not a separate Entity, but a unified wholistic energy that encompasses everything and everyone in the Universe. In truth, we are all One. When we believe this, it becomes our experience, and we have achieved a major breakthrough.

We can be certain to feel joy when we are giving or receiving unconditional love and support, and this will never change. It is part of the human condition and the solution to all our problems. In our consciousness, God represents everyone and everything. When God becomes our friend, so will everyone else.

God Within

The energy of friendship and support that God is, is ever available to us. I call it my inner self. In order to feel the support of my inner self, I simply have to open myself to it and absolutely trust that it is, indeed, supporting me.

29
The Feeling Exercise

In order to achieve a life that works perfectly, we each have to decide what a perfect life is. "Perfect" is a word that has a different meaning for each person. We have been taught to believe that a perfect life is one in which we receive things we wish to have, such as vacations, raises in pay, a better job, a new car, a bigger house, or more money in the bank. Our focus is invariably on the world around us. When the world acts friendly and generously to us, we are happy.

The truth is that the world is a big mirror. It is always reflecting back to us the state of our consciousness. The world feels fine when we feel fine.

Our current belief systems generate many reasons to interpret our circumstances and the behavior of people we encounter in a way that leads us to feel frustrated, annoyed, depressed, angry, or sad. Refraining from responding to the events and people around us in this judgmental way is a greater challenge than we realize. For not only were we all taught to judge people and events, but we were taught to use traditional standards of good and bad. We were also taught to judge the quality of our lives by the conditions that occur around us and to us. Moving into a space of totally loving these people and these conditions goes against our basic beliefs. Yet loving them is our only salvation.

Emotions are feelings distorted by the thoughts that we have attached to the feelings (see chapter 15). These thoughts include beliefs that it is dangerous to feel and express these feelings. These thoughts also include beliefs that it is dangerous to feel and use the power that lies behind these feelings.

We are now in the process of allowing these feelings and this power to arise within us. In order to feel these feelings free of the fears that induced their suppression, and free of the beliefs that distorted them, we must first feel them just the way they are, distorted as they may be, and fearful as they may seem. The feeling exercise described below supports that process. Each of these feelings in its undistorted form and free of fear is some aspect of joyfulness. Joyfulness has an infinite range. However, joyfulness cannot be experienced unless our underlying state of being is peaceful. Joyfulness, the feeling quality of love, and peacefulness are Siamese twins. They are inseparable. Once we feel peaceful, we know we are joyful.

Joyfulness can be inspiring and entertaining, contemplative and calm, compassionate and caring, or persuasive and compelling. There is no limitation to the range of its qualities.

We can practice feeling our feelings just as they are. This will increase our trust in ourselves and in other people so that eventually we shall be able to feel all of our feelings fully, freely, and without fear and distortion. Then we shall recognize that every feeling is essentially joyful and an experience of deep connection to the essence of everyone.

 THE FEELING EXERCISE

Close your eyes and scan your body. Notice how you are feeling. Then:
1. Feel the feeling free of any thoughts you have about it.
2. Feel love for the feeling just the way it is.
3. Feel love for yourself having that feeling.

When you are able to feel the feeling free of any thoughts you have connected to the feeling, you will notice the energy behind the feeling. There is enormous power in the energy behind our feelings.

When we release that energy by feeling our feelings free of the judgments we have trained ourselves to attach to them, the energy is available to us to support our creativity. We have within us, at all times, the energy and the creativity to live a life that is truly unconditionally self-supportive.

Life is a feeling experience. We feel with our hearts. When we open our hearts, which is done by releasing judgments, we give ourselves the joy of feeling all the ways that we love ourselves, others, and the world around us. When we open our hearts, we also feel peaceful.

By doing the Feeling Exercise every day, we have an opportunity to expand our feeling of and appreciation for peacefulness. Peacefulness is the doorway through which we gain access to the beauty, the aliveness, the wonder, and the inspiration that life is all about.

Peacefulness is in each of us. Making peace with everyone and everything as we go through our day helps us to expand this basic energy force within us. Remember, peacefulness is an aspect of love, which is an aspect of joyfulness. Focusing on any one of them puts us in touch with the others.

Since many of us have buried joyfulness deep within, we must continue to make peace with the layers of illusion that cover it until it shines forth continuously. Each day that we do the Feeling Exercise, we release more joyfulness.

Through this exercise, we awaken feelings, and we begin to see that the judgments and fears we have had about these feelings are no longer relevant to our here and now. We realize that without the judgments and fears, all our feelings are experienced as joyfulness and love.

Question: What if I am feeling angry? How do I feel joyful if I am mad at someone?

Answer: Anger is the result of a repression of your feelings. We have all repressed many of our feelings. This came about when we concluded, in our early years, that in order to survive we had to accept the belief systems of our parents and other authority figures. Furthermore, when we repressed our feelings, we also repressed our power, for *our power resides in our feelings.* Therefore, whenever we believe it is unsafe to freely feel our feelings, we block our power.

The expansion of consciousness that we are all witnessing and experiencing brings these repressed feelings to the surface. This is a scary process because the fear that induced the original repression of these feelings comes to the surface along with the desire to feel the feelings. Yet, as long as we remain too afraid to fully and freely feel our feelings and the power behind them, we keep creating outer conflicts that reflect the inner conflict between the part of us that wishes to freely feel and express its feelings and the part of us that represses these feelings out of fear for the retaliation that such free expression may bring.

Our lives are so filled with these outer conflicts, we have come to believe that the only way to have an intense feeling is to create some form of conflict. Thus, we appear late for appointments, insult another, or in an infinite number of other ways create experiences that intensify the feelings in our bodies.

What we are ready to learn is that we can experience the intensity of our feelings without the dramatic circumstances that we normally create to induce them. The practical problem that we face is that we have already created many dramatic conflicts in our lives, believe they are real, and find it hard to release them. The Feeling Exercise (page 124) helps us to feel these repressed feelings and to release the energy locked in them. Regular use of this exercise offers a simple way to open us to our feelings, open our feelings to us, and at the same time reduce the need to create outer conflicts in our lives.

For those who have used the Feeling Exercise to release energy that was locked up in anger toward someone and who now wish to proceed toward a loving relationship with that person, you may use the following exercise:

DEEP LOVING EXERCISE

Introductory Comments: In order to reach a place where you can feel deep love for someone, you must first release all judgment, reclaim all open-heart energy you have invested in finding fault with the person, and finally, feel deep forgiveness (deep forgiveness is akin to deep love). You also need the support of your inner self.

Your inner self is the part of you that is connected to Infinite Intelligence. This inner self creates your life the way it is. It brings into your life the people it does so that you may feel love for them precisely as they are. When you are able to feel love for them, you free the energy that is repressed by your judgment. This enables your inner self to accomplish its purpose in bringing these people to you.

Take your time with each step. Do not proceed to the next step until you have completed the step you are on.

1. I ask my inner self to assist me in releasing all the judgments that I have about _____. (Feel the judgments dissolve.)

2. I ask my inner self to assist me in reclaiming all the open-heart energy that I have invested in finding fault with _____. (Begin to feel that open-heart energy return to you. Deeply feel that energy, claiming it as your own. Deeply feel it again.)

3. Feel deep love for your inner self.

4. I ask my inner self to assist me in feeling deep forgiveness for _____. (Feel the deep forgiveness.)

5. I ask my inner self to assist me in feeling deep love for _____. (Feel the deep love and embrace the person in that deeply felt love.)

127

After you have released judgment of the person, reclaimed your open-heart energy, felt deep forgiveness and then deep love, you can appreciate that feeling deep love for the person is infinitely more pleasurable and much more fun than feeling angry at him. You realize that you don't have to create intense conflicts in your life to enjoy the intensity of your feelings.

Feeling deep love for another and for yourself is a very intense experience and one that you can enjoy as often as you wish—just for the fun of it.

30
The Game of Life and How to Play It

To become proficient at a game requires a clear understanding of the rules of that game. It also requires a clear intention to achieve mastery or proficiency. The game of life has the same requirement as any other game. Preparing to play soccer by buying a rule book on baseball is not helpful. The reason that many people do not enjoy a high quality of life is that they are not certain what the real game is and have not mastered the rules of that game.

In this book I describe the real game and also outline and explain the rules for you. Once you agree with the rules and choose to play the game, the results you achieve are then dependent on your intention to succeed. As soon as you make this kind of commitment to yourself, the Universe will acknowledge your intention immediately and will give you such generous support that the quality of your life will improve substantially and will continue to improve with each step you take.

There is no limit to the amount you can improve the quality of your life. No matter how wonderful it might seem at any level you have achieved, the possibility of further improvement always exists, and the game never ends.

Playing the real game is fun wherever and whenever you do it. It is as much fun for a beginner as it is for an advanced player. Think of any activity you love to participate in. Your level of skill is not as important as is the joy of participation. A child who loves to play baseball receives as much pleasure playing on a sandlot as a superstar does playing in a major league stadium.

Start playing the real game right away and allow yourself the pleasure and enjoyment that comes from playing the one game that offers a feeling of fulfillment to each and every player. Just listen to your intuition. Our Coach never gives a wrong signal and always lovingly encourages, supports, and inspires all of Her players.

The next concept is one that explains what we can expect when we shift from one career to another.

31
Owning the Level

Once we have achieved mastery of anything in our lives, we own the level attained by that achievement. What's more, the skills used to attain that level are transferable. We see illustrations of this principle all the time.

Look at the business section of your newspaper and you will often see that a president of a major corporation has transferred to another major corporation whose product or service is totally different from the product or service of the company that he left. Once a person functions at a presidential level, he owns that level and moves around in society at that level.

In our society, we use a hierarchical system to rate various skills and talents. A person who is talented in business or in a profession is usually accorded a higher status than one whose talent is in sewing, cooking, repairing appliances, or hanging wallpaper, and it remains that way as long as the people involved accept the existing standard. Yet each talent is truly equal in value to every other talent. And anyone with a skill or talent that is not usually accorded high status and value has a relatively simple remedy. Far more important than the value placed by society on a skill or talent is the value placed on it by the individual with the skill or talent.

When our perception of the value of our talent increases, so will the actual value of it to others.

The person who sews, knits, or cooks with great skill is entitled to the same acknowledgment as is the successful president of a major corporation. Each of us is entitled to be treated as a superstar. However, *others always treat us in the way that we treat ourselves. Until we view ourselves and what we do as important and valuable, no one else will.*

In our area of talent, we are all potential superstars. Since, along with every talent come the tools to express it perfectly, we can become superstars when we are ready. And others will view us as superstars when we view ourselves that way.

Question: Are you saying that once we have achieved some success at any one thing, the skills and consciousness developed to attain that success are transferable?

Answer: That is exactly what I am saying. Many people express their talents at very high levels of performance, yet they do not acknowledge themselves for what they have accomplished. This is often the case with those who express their talents as avocations, such as sewing or knitting exquisitely, or repairing appliances expertly.

Each of us is given one or more talents. When we are in touch with our real selves through the full and free expression of our talents, our whole life experience is different. The perfection of the Universe is such that it is intended for our lives to work perfectly, with ease and simplicity. When we lead from our talents, we find out that such a life is possible.

Another way of viewing who we really are is to recognize that each of us is a genius when it comes to expressing our personal talent or talents. Why not allow ourselves to be the geniuses we truly are, and receive all the joy that expressing oneself as a genius allows?

On a practical level, this means that when our career focus and talents merge, we can expect to reach a level of success that is equivalent to the greatest success we have enjoyed to date. In fact, as we integrate the principles, we can expect to go to a much higher level. For the creative and loving energy released by our alignment with the Universe will remarkably improve the quality of our life on all levels.

Question: I am an artist. I work with clay. My pieces are of excellent quality, and I receive constant acknowledgment for the quality of my work. How do I support myself until I earn enough from this talent?

Answer: There are a few separate issues to notice. First, keep your present source of income to allow you to be comfortable financially. Express your talent in your spare time. As you clear your energy around money, you will also be creating interest in your works of art.

Next, look at your present life. How successful are you in dealing with money? In other words, what level do you own? If you are comfortable with money and it moves easily in your life right now, then you can expect that to continue as you move into your new career.

On the other hand, if you experience uncertainty and problems with money, expect this to continue until you expand your consciousness. Remember, *we always experience in the physical world an exact outplaying of the state of our consciousness.* If your present situation with money is less than comfortable, take the time to make peace with money. See chapters 11, 14, and 37 for suggestions on how to open to abundance in your life.

Be patient. Take small steps and celebrate each successful step you take. Use your support group to keep your focus on these issues.

Also, remember that the Universe is on your side. You enlist Its support by using principle. Ask for Its support and then feel Its support constantly. If you do not feel this support, it means that you are not giving

133

yourself support. This is another way of saying that you do not feel good about yourself and thus are not worthy of your own or anyone else's support.

32
Inside Out

Trying to change the world around us is not only exhausting, the results never give us more than temporary pleasure. Most of us spend our entire lives changing things in our environment in an effort to improve the quality of our lives. We seek more money, newer and fancier cars, more expensive houses, and more beautiful clothes as ways to make us feel better.

The pleasure brought by this approach cannot last, since it results from a belief that is contrary to our reason for being. We are not here to accumulate things or to amass wealth. *We are here to serve one another by giving generously of our talents and rendering services or creating products that express these talents. The natural result of this process is that money and other material wealth flows into our lives.*

We often reverse this process and make money the primary motivating factor. Seeking money or other material things invariably puts us in a position where we fail to support other people through the expression of our talents. The Universe never misses an opportunity to remind us of our priorities. The reminder comes in the form of a feeling of discomfort. The irony is that we can have all the things we require to enjoy a life that works perfectly, provided we reorder our priorities.

Our first priority is to master the basic laws of the Universe. This will bring about the inner changes that will attract more abundance than we ever dreamed possible. When we trust the Universe, we find that abundance is our natural state of being, and that perfect things flow into our life, just as we need them.

My experience has taught me that in the process of integrating universal principles into our consciousness, the core issues in our lives rise to the surface, so that we can see them clearly and make peace with them. For example, if as a child you were told over and over again that you will never amount to anything, or that you are not a responsible person when it comes to handling money, or that life is a series of setbacks that you must make the best of, you *will* create circumstances to remind you that you have not yet expanded these limited beliefs. Until you do reperceive them, they will override your ability to allow the natural abundance of the Universe to flow into your life.

Understanding the definition of abundance is only the first step. It is not the last. After you understand the concept of abundance and agree with it, you then start the process of becoming aware of all the beliefs you hold that are contrary to that concept.

In order to simplify the release process, you must be patient. Be gentle and kind to yourself and take as long as you require to forgive the people in your life who exhibited behavior or taught you things that you believe were unloving and unsupportive of you. Know that every little step you take in forgiving these people is really a big step in your life. Perseverance does pay off.

A most self-supportive step to take is to join a universal principles support group (see chapter 42). This will ensure that you experience unconditional love and support as you proceed with what might seem like a painful process—feeling forgiveness for significant people in your life. In fact, every time you feel a little more forgiveness for anyone, you release pain. Pain is the result of your unwillingness to feel forgiveness for these people.

Finally, remember that your willingness to feel forgiveness for these people represents your willingness to forgive yourself. We are in this game of life together. Everything that we do in support of another is really a way that we support ourselves.

33
Criteria and Standards

What are your criteria for a successful life? As human beings we are so created that we require standards or criteria as guidelines for our life. The society in which we live encourages us to adopt material wealth, status, physical beauty, and competitiveness as our standards. Since society introduces these criteria to us in our formative years, we tend to adopt them without being conscious of the impact they have on our lives.

When we adopt these criteria, they become our beliefs. These beliefs, as the eyes through which we see our world, determine how we interpret the events of our life. This, in turn, establishes the quality of our experiences with these events.

Fortunately, the Universe is not a passive bystander. While It gives each of us the choice to adopt whatever standards we wish, It also establishes the consequences for the choices we make. The Universe truly wants us to be at peace with ourselves, and so It continues to signal us every time we make a choice.

We were each created for a purpose. That purpose is not to accumulate wealth, achieve status, and compete with one another. Selection of criteria such as these invariably results in experiences of discomfort.

There is a simple solution to this apparent problem, and that is to adopt different criteria for our lives. By selecting the criteria of universal principles—such as forgiveness, harmony, inner peace, and unconditional love (each one being an aspect of the other)—we place ourselves in alignment with the Universe and open ourselves to Its abundant support. Once we adopt any one of these criteria, we reap the benefits of all of them, since they are all aspects of each other. In other words, we guarantee that we will have it all.

Built into the human species is the need to give and receive unconditional love. It is something that is an integral part of us. Wherever we look for unconditional love we find it, and whenever we express it we improve the quality of our lives.

Seeing the perfection in ourselves and everyone around us is a way we express unconditional love. It also opens us to fully and freely express who we really are.

Question: What you are saying seems logical and yet it appears too simple. Am I to understand that all we have to do is to focus all our attention on the perfection of what is presently happening and everything else will be taken care of?

Answer: Yes. That is the beauty and the simplicity of dealing with the highest thoughts. Remember, the Universe already functions perfectly. We, as a product of that perfect Universe, are created to function perfectly. Believing this is a choice that we make. The Universe continually signals us how we can move into alignment with It, but It will not make the choice for us. As soon as we realize that the real game allows all of us to feel loved, supported, and fulfilled, and that in fact the Universe guarantees it, the only decision left is whether or not to play the real game.

We do not have to do anything to make ourselves perfect—we already are perfect. Our life experience is the opportunity to release all beliefs that we are less than perfect, right now. The more we allow ourselves to believe in our perfection, the more we open ourselves to the abundance of the Universe. It wants to

138

flow through our lives. It is we who either keep abundance out or let it in.

It is time for a break.

34
How to Accept the Results We Are Creating

The law of cause and effect tells us that we always receive what we want. When we notice that we are getting results that seem unsatisfactory, we must first recognize that what we now have is what we want, even though we think that we want something else. The knowing part of us directs us to these experiences or attracts them to us to help us recognize that we are in conflict with something and are resisting or avoiding making peace with it.

Our next point of focus is to make peace with the situation just the way it is. In order to do this, we often need to remind ourselves that no situation or person is bad or good, right or wrong. Developing the willingness to release these previously made judgments, which we are holding on to, can sometimes take a lot of patience and perseverance.

We are now ready to replace the prior want with the desire to experience inner peace. It is only through the doorway of inner peace that we find our creativity and the inspiration to express it in a way that supports us and everyone who may enjoy and benefit from our creative expression.

Finding inner peace and through it the expression of our creativity puts us in touch with who we really are. We come to recognize that we are valuable and essential parts of a larger experience that binds each of us to everyone else—a large mutual support system comprising many smaller support systems. What each of us truly wants is to feel the nurturing warmth and the inspirational creativity of this love-based mutual support system. It is perfectly natural for all of us to live in harmony with everyone else. In fact, no one wants anything else more than this.

35
Means and Ends

The result you achieve is the method you select to arrive at the result.

To achieve inner peace, focus on inner peace and act peacefully, moment by moment.

To achieve unconditional love, focus on unconditional love and act unconditionally loving, moment by moment.

To achieve a life that works perfectly, focus on perfection and see the perfection in yourself and everyone else, moment by moment.

To experience total abundance in your life, see and feel the abundance all around you, moment by moment.

The principle is simple. Means and ends are always identical.

36
Resolving Problems

The major obstacle to resolving problems in our lives is our attempt to deal with them as though they are something outside of us. The truth is that every problem is an outward manifestation of our state of consciousness. When our consciousness is clear and at peace, the problem disappears.

Every attempt we make to resolve a problem by changing something outside of ourselves will be unsuccessful. Changing our circumstances might temporarily ease the situation, but the problem cannot be released until there is an expansion of consciousness.

An example illustrates the principle involved. Assume you owe someone $1,000.00. She is demanding payment, and you have only $100.00 cash on hand. Attempts to raise $900.00 by borrowing or working overtime can partially solve the problem but it is not until you look at the problem from a higher perspective that you recognize that you created the debt and the lack of funds to repay it on time. Understanding that you want the problem and the accompanying discomfort is the first step to its complete solution. Also, realizing that you want to withhold money from this particular creditor is an essential next step. The final clearing of your consciousness comes when you can feel the desire to freely and happily benefit the creditor. Once this occurs, the funds to do it will appear, or the creditor may forgive the debt.

Remember, the world around us teaches us about the state of our consciousness. We literally create all of our problems, and they do not disappear until we clear our consciousness of the conflict represented by the problem.

What we consider our toughest problems are just reflections of those issues that we have the most resistance to resolving. Another way of stating this is that we would rather experience discomfort by continuing with the problem than to release the discomfort by allowing ourselves to feel love for another person. Ultimately, we recognize that other person as ourselves.

37
Opening to More Abundance

Acknowledge All of the Abundance You Already Have

Give thanks for your friends and family. Give thanks for the trees, sun, beaches, rivers, mountains, and birds. Give thanks for the food you eat, the clothes you wear, your house or apartment, your car, the money in your pocket and in the bank. This is a wonderful exercise. It is so simple and it is so powerful. There is a basic principle operating each time you do this. The principle is: Whatever you focus your thoughts on expands. The more you notice and acknowledge all that you have, the more you open yourself to receive.

The converse is also true. If you dwell upon what you do not have, you put energy into scarcity and you will experience more of it. This is a simple principle and one well worth mastering. Understand that anything less than abundance is an illusion. Scarcity is an illusion. The natural state of the Universe is abundance. When you are not experiencing abundance, you are pushing it away from yourself. As you practice acknowledging and giving thanks for all that you have, you will break up the old pattern and replace it with one that puts you in alignment with the abundance of the Universe.

Spend More Time Doing What You Love

Doing what you love is an expression of your talent. Your talent and creativity are two gifts that have been given to you as an expression of the abundance of the Universe. When used in conjunction with each other, there is no limit to the further abundance you can create for yourself.

Do the Feeling Exercise

Doing the Feeling Exercise is a wonderful way to release the energy (power) that is bound up in your feelings. Feeling your feelings fully and consistently puts you in touch with this power. It is a peaceful power and expresses itself as inspiration, which together with your creativity leads you to a new understanding of abundance (see chapter 29).

Participate in a Support Group

Participation in a support group allows you to interact with others who love and support you unconditionally. It is the best environment in which to expand your vision, feel your feelings, and practice the basic principles. The more ways you find to create support in expanding your vision, feeling your feelings, and using the basic principles, the simpler your life will become.

Be aware that you cannot give to others what you have not allowed yourself to receive. So be generous and kind to yourself. You deserve it. Then give freely to others, as you allow others to continue to give freely to you.

Notice What Works for You and Continue Doing It

Forget about *why* things are the way they are. This is irrelevant. Just notice *how* they are now. When you notice something that makes you feel comfortable, enjoy it and do it often. Be careful not to misinterpret this. I am referring to a deep feeling of satisfaction and peacefulness that encompasses you and those around you.

Others Do Not Support You More Than You Support Yourself

You are a transmitting and receiving station. Your beliefs create the signals that you send out. If you believe that you are not worth much, you send signals to other people to withhold their love and support from you. The solution is to notice how you really feel about yourself. If you are uncertain how you really feel about yourself, just become aware of how others act toward you. They are accurately reflecting the signals you are emitting.

To improve the way you feel about yourself, you can practice a simple mirror exercise. Look at yourself in the mirror. Notice how you feel about yourself. Keep looking directly at yourself until you feel deep love.

The best way to prepare yourself for the mirror exercise is to do the Feeling Exercise (see chapter 29). That exercise will open your energy field and make it easier to access the love that is within.

38
Meditation

One of the best ways to learn to distinguish between what is real and what is an illusion is through the practice of meditation. This is quiet time devoted to contemplating our real selves and our relationship to God. We cannot spend too much time reminding ourselves of this relationship. This is also the time when we remind ourselves that our spiritual being is real and that it is connected to all other beings.

Another benefit of meditation is that it helps us to achieve a state of relaxation. It is only when we are relaxed that we can be truly creative and fully and freely express who we really are. We allow ourselves to relax when we believe that whatever is perfect for us is a gift from the Universe, awaiting our readiness to receive it.

Meditation also provides an opportunity to be in touch with the motivating factor, the life force behind the infinite supply of energy in the Universe, that which connects and supports all of us—love. Fear, anxiety, or any other emotional state is simply the result of our withholding love from ourselves and others. When we are in such an emotional state, we create a tension that precludes feeling love.

Our major misperception is the belief that the world, as we experience it, is real. When we meditate, we remind ourselves to align with the Universe and allow Its love to flow through us as the source of our creativity and our sustenance.

39
Safety

There is total safety in the Universe at all times. We feel that safety when we are unconditionally loving and supporting another person, or receiving unconditional love and support—in other words, when we are in touch with what is real in us and others, and with the Universe.

We do not have to do anything to save ourselves or the Universe. Furthermore, acting out of a sense of urgency does not lead to high-quality performance. When we feel the peace of the Universe, we can express fully and freely who we really are in ways that truly support everyone.

Our essence, and the essence of everything else in the Universe, cannot die. Until we believe that, our life experience is one of continual fear of death. Our essence is eternal, knows that it is, and is willing to support us in being constantly aware of this truth. Until we believe that we are eternal, we live in continual fear that something bad, terrible, or painful can happen to us at any time.

Since our essence cannot experience pain or death, we have the potential to express who we really are and live a life of joy forever. The choice is always ours.

Remember, when you are ready, *you can have it all.*

40
Asking for Support in Consciousness

The game of life is played at the level of consciousness. Whatever manifests itself on the physical level is a result of the state of our consciousness. Almost every one of us was taught the opposite. We believe that if we are dissatisfied with what is occurring in the physical sphere, we can just step in and change it. If we are unhappy with a relationship, we change partners. If we feel unappreciated at work, we look for another job.

It is important to be aware of the fact that until we expand our consciousness, all the changes that we make on the physical level are superficial rather than real. The person who changes partners or changes jobs soon learns that the new partner bothers him in the same way that the first one did or that the new job creates the same discomfort that the old one did. The faces and the settings may change, but the underlying dynamics remain the same. In order to create a change of substance, try the following:

Remind yourself that your consciousness is the point of focus.

Become aware that the result you are achieving is what you presently believe and want; in fact, the knowing part of you is guiding you into this experience to enable you to make peace with it just the way it is.

Ask yourself if you are truly ready to expand your vision. If you are, locate a principle that applies to the issue that you are dealing with.

Then frame a request for support in consciousness—that is, a request in terms of principle using the present tense.

For example, assume your boss is making demands on you that you feel are excessive and unreasonable. You have complained to your friends and family and have described many faults that you see in your boss. Requests for support in consciousness can be as follows:

I ask for support in consciousness in not finding fault with my boss, *or*

I ask for support in consciousness in feeling forgiveness for my boss, *or*

I ask for support in consciousness in feeling gratitude for all the positive qualities I see in my boss, *or*

I ask for support in consciousness in feeling more loving and supportive of myself, recognizing that others will feel good about me when I feel good about myself.

Consider another example. You are having a great deal of difficulty paying your bills on time. You have more current debts than current income. Some suggested requests for support in consciousness are:

I ask for support in consciousness in remembering that my consciousness is the point of focus and that until I expand my consciousness the results I achieve will not change in any beneficial way, *or*

I ask for support in consciousness in being at peace with my shortage of income and loving it unconditionally just the way it is, *or*

I ask for support in consciousness in feeling good about my creditors and developing a desire to give generously to them, *or*

I ask for support in consciousness in seeing my creditors as myself and feeling my love for them as love for myself, *or*

I ask for support in consciousness in believing that abundance is the natural state of affairs in the Universe and feeling my resistance to abundance so that I can release this resistance, *or*

I ask for support in consciousness in feeling grateful for all the abundance I presently have and opening myself to allow more of this abundance into my life so that I may share it generously with others.

It is helpful to make requests for support in consciousness to yourself. However, the impact is greater when these requests are made at a support group meeting. (See the section "Make Individual Requests for Specific Support,"on page 171, in chapter 42.) Such requests are to be made spontaneously, since they are most useful when they reflect the true desire of the presenter at the moment the request is made.

Listen carefully to your request. Notice the amount of intention you have when you make your request. You may be surprised to hear how weak your request sounds, even though you thought you really wanted what you were requesting.

If your request has less than a 100 percent intention behind it, and you feel you really wish to have what you are asking for, then ask again at subsequent support group meetings. Continue asking until you feel that you have reached 100 percent intention and that you are clearly communicating that level of intention to the group.

Let's take another break.

41
Group Purpose and Alignment

There is no more important preliminary activity for a group (two or more persons) to focus on than defining their purpose for being together. The resulting statement becomes the group purpose. In the same way that a person's individual purpose creates the inspiration for her life, the group purpose creates the inspiration for the life of the group.

When there is a clear alignment in purpose among the participants, each moves forward in the activities of the group with total confidence. It is well worth the time it takes to define the group purpose and clarify each member's alignment with the group before proceeding with the formalization of the group.

A simple way to define a group purpose is for each participant in a group to separately define her purpose for the group. Then the participants share their purposes with each other. Next, the group creates a single statement of group purpose. This is done with everyone's participation, at a group meeting. Although there is no need to rush to complete the statement defining the group purpose, it should remain a priority item on the agenda at each meeting until it is completed.

Nothing is more valuable to the participants than having a clearly defined group purpose that inspires every member of the group. In fact, without such a purpose, there is little reason for the group to continue to meet. The creation of a group purpose that inspires each member assures the success of the group.

We live our lives at the level of consciousness. Defining our purpose in universal terms aligns us with the power of the Universe. It is the Universe working through us that creates wonderful results. Our sole function is to keep ourselves in alignment with the Universe. When a group aligns with the Universe, the power expressed through the group is expanded enormously. Every member of the group not only feels this power but also enjoys the confidence and certainty that this power brings.

The foregoing recommendations apply to a group that is about to form. Existing groups should approach alignment in an entirely different way. When a person is in an existing group, be it a marriage, a social club, a business venture, or any other kind of group, it is most helpful to look at the group in terms of the Three Steps (see chapter 46).

First, recognize that you are in the situation because you created it. If the situation is uncomfortable, remind yourself that your experience with the group reflects the present state of your consciousness.

Second, feel love for yourself just the way you are. You cannot feel love for another just the way that person is if you don't first feel love for yourself just the way you are. This leads you to the Feeling Exercise (chapter 29).

Third, don't judge yourself or others in the group. This locks the energy within you. If you notice any judgment on your part, try practicing forgiveness for all those whom you are judging. Continue the practice daily until all judgment is released. Then shift the focus to feeling unconditional love for the other group member(s). Remember, whenever we judge another, we are really judging a part of ourselves. When we finally feel unconditional love for the other person, we come to love a part of ourselves from which we previously withheld love.

Doing the Three Steps in connection with existing relationships enables you to come to peace with these relationships. It is when you are at peace that you appreciate the value and purpose of these relationships.

Let's assume that your present group experience is a job that you perceive as being less than perfect. Following the foregoing procedure will lead to one of two probable outcomes: Either you find that having come to peace with the people involved, the job is now wonderful, or you are led to another job.

Every group has the potential to be a perfect support group. Even if you are the only one in the group who is willing to see the others as perfect just the way they are, that willingness on your part is sufficient to improve the energy of the group in a very significant way. Others will respond to your broader vision.

Our alignments with others reflect our alignment with the Universe. Time is not a factor. It is helpful to be patient and to allow as long as it takes to bring ourselves into alignment with others. But it is important to focus on alignment continually in order to sustain the forward movement. All of this is done at the level of consciousness. As changes occur at this level, they will be reflected in our daily experiences.

One of the greatest tools for improving our alignments is the definition of group purpose. Whenever there is discomfort within a group, it means either that there is no group purpose, that group purpose is not being defined at a universal level, or that one or more of the participants is not aligned with that purpose.

Whether or not there is alignment with purpose, it is helpful for as many participants as possible to express unconditional love and support for each other. Unconditional love and support means seeing the person as perfect just the way she is. Loving unconditionally means recognizing that if another person's behavior is bothersome, that behavior represents a part of ourselves that we are not accepting and loving just the way it is.

Do not confuse unconditional love and support with the need to do anything outwardly. It is not an obligation to give money, spend time with someone, or do anything in particular, although it can result in an outward action. But in order to be beneficial to all parties, that action must be inspired and totally voluntary, not something done out of a sense of obligation.

In summary, then, the definition and redefinition of group purpose is the single most valuable activity for any group to experience.

161

Having an inspiring group purpose and redefining it from time to time, as may be necessary, guarantees not only success for the group, but success for the participants as well, beyond their activities in the group.

42
Support

The Universe functions as a mutual support system. Everything in the Universe relates to and influences everything else. The sun provides the energy for growth of plants, which in turn provide food for animals. The planets exert gravitational influences on each other. Our use of the resources on our planet affects the quality of the air we breathe and the water we drink. Every thought and feeling each of us has vibrates through the physical universe. We are all part of a mutual support system.

Our ability to function successfully within a mutual support system is related to our willingness to recognize and believe that this is indeed the nature of our life. Society often teaches us differently. It encourages us to strike out on our own and work to achieve personal objectives and goals. We are left with the impression that we can achieve happiness at the expense of others, or at least without caring about others.

It is important to keep reminding ourselves that each of us is an essential and important part of a system of mutual support. Unless we are ever mindful of the interrelatedness of each and every person and thing in the Universe, we cannot enjoy the benefit of the perfect design of our universal system.

The basic laws of the Universe are the guidelines for life within this mutual support system. Following these laws places us in alignment with everyone and everything within the system.

We see this system functioning, to varying degrees, within families, clubs, associations, religious organizations, and businesses.

When we forget about our interrelatedness, we establish rules and standards for groups that are not in alignment with the basic laws of the Universe. We have all noticed groups that do not select as their primary purpose the creation of a nurturing and harmonious environment for all their participants.

But it is possible for people everywhere to create nurturing and harmonious support groups for themselves. The following five guidelines will enable a group of people (a group is two or more) to begin the process of forming a mutual support group.

Five Guidelines for Forming a Support Group

1. *Define the group purpose.*

   The group purpose aligns the energy within the group and inspires the participants to move in the direction of the group purpose. It creates trust among the participants and an eagerness to expand their experience of mutual support.

2. *See the perfection in everything.*

   This is a reminder that we experience everything the way we perceive it. There is no event that is good or bad, right or wrong (see chapter 13).

3. *Speak in the present tense.*

   The only time that ever exists is the present moment. (The past is gone forever and the future is yet to be.) By allowing everything that is a part of our present moment to be perfect just the way it is, we support ourselves in being at peace in the present moment. It is through this state of peacefulness that we feel the connectedness of everything with everything else and the beauty of each present moment. By stating our thoughts in the present tense, we remind ourselves that only the present moment exists.

4. *Make a conscious attempt to support one another.*

Remember that we are part of a mutual support system. We are all dependent upon one another. As we support each other, we support ourselves. We come together as a self-selected family to learn how to feel unconditional love for ourselves and for each other. Once we learn how to love unconditionally in our support group, we can bring this ability to every relationship in our lives.

5. *Remind each other gently, kindly, and lovingly of these guidelines when they are not being observed.*

These five guidelines serve to launch a support group. Additional guidelines are needed, however, to sustain the focus and positive energy of a group whenever a participant presents a personal problem.

The Eleven Steps outlined on the next page provide additional guidance in such a situation and are used primarily in the context of a support group meeting. These steps contain suggestions and questions that enable the presenter to reperceive his problem in terms of universal principles.

To increase the effectiveness of the procedure, the other participants remain silent while the presenter speaks. It is an active silence, however, with each person focusing attention on and support for the presenter. There is no outward response by the participants. If a listener agrees with what the presenter says, he is not to smile his approval and encouragement, or if he disagrees with something said he is not to shake his head or in any other way exhibit his disapproval. If a listener does disagree with or feels uncomfortable about something the presenter is saying or doing, it is a perfect opportunity for the listener to release his judgment of the situation and to practice being unconditionally loving. The major function of each listener is to provide so much love and support for the presenter that he feels free to say what is true for him at that moment. *At no time during or after the exercise is anyone to discuss the situation with the presenter.*

165

Insights into his situation will continue to unfold to the presenter as long as the energy of the exercise is not disrupted by any outside influences. The insights gained by the presenter during and after this exercise will prove invaluable in assisting with the resolution of the situation.

The Eleven Steps
(Procedure to Reperceive a Problem)

When a participant in the support group is facing a situation that is causing him discomfort, the following step-by-step procedure is suggested. A member of the group reads the instructions, one at a time, allowing the person with the problem to respond to each instruction before proceeding to the next one.

1. *Define the situation.*

   The presenter explains, as briefly as possible, what is causing his discomfort.

2. *Close your eyes and become aware of the feeling in your body, separate from any thoughts you may have about it. Indicate when the discomfort leaves.*

   The person is encouraged to separate the feeling in his body from all thoughts he may have about it. Chapter 15, on emotion, explains the importance of this exercise. As long as a thought is attached to a feeling, the discomfort remains.

3. *Do you agree that nothing you or anyone else has done or is doing is either wrong or right? Please explain.*

   The presenter is reminded that as long as he is judging himself or anyone else, he will be locked in the discomfort he is presently experiencing. The only way to release the discomfort is to release all judgment of everything and everyone, including himself.

4. *Do you realize that you are receiving exactly what you want and the other person is receiving exactly what he wants? Please explain.*

Here we recall the law of cause and effect (see chapter 7).

5. *Do you recognize that the way you see the other person is really the way you see yourself? Can you give an example?*

Noticing the ways in which another person is not perfect just the way he is reminds the presenter that he is still judging himself in the same way.

6. *Do you realize that what you are experiencing is precisely how you see the situation?*

The way the presenter sees others or situations is a reflection of his own state of consciousness. It is the most efficient way to find out what he really believes.

7. *Perceive the **same** situation differently. Create another interpretation of it.*

Everything we experience is a result of our perception of it. When we are able to reperceive a situation, our experience of it transforms. In order for a person to perceive a troubling situation in a different way, he must let go of his attachment to his present perception of the situation. It is his unwillingness to do this that has given rise to the situation in the first place. If, after a couple of minutes, the presenter is unable to perceive the same situation differently, he is told to continue with this step at home. The presenter may then proceed to the next step.

(*Author's Note:* My experience has taught me that while suggestions from others in the group as to how the presenter can perceive the same situation differently may appear to benefit the presenter, in the long run only the presenter's self-initiated reperception of the situation is of lasting benefit. Therefore, listeners are not to make any suggestions to the presenter either during or after the exercise.)

8. *Are you willing to see and feel the perfection of what is just the way it is? Can you feel the personal power that comes to you when you accept this as your purpose?*

9. *Describe the ways you are withholding love from yourself and others.*

   All discomfort involves a withholding of love. Locating the withholding of love helps to clarify what is really going on.

10. *Go behind the apparent circumstances of the situation and locate the love in yourself and in all others involved in the situation.*

    The only true motivation for all behavior is love. When anyone's behavior appears less than loving, it is just the closest that the person can come at that moment to expressing love.

11. *Feel the joy that comes when the love is found and expressed.*

    This puts a person in touch with what is always within him, if he is willing to look for it.

When using the Eleven Steps, one of the participants in the group acts as the leader and guides the person with a problem through the procedure. The other group members listen attentively, making no outward response but feeling as much unconditional love for the presenter as they can offer. This supports the presenter in learning what he really believes about the issues raised by each step in the process.

Learning the truth about our beliefs is the first step in reperceiving them. When we truly understand that we have created our beliefs, we know that only we have the capacity to expand our view of them and thus release the power bound up in them.

The foregoing five guidelines, the Eleven Steps, and the suggested outline for a typical support group meeting (see next page) are designed to keep the participants of a support group in alignment with universal principles. A support group gives each participant the opportunity to practice the principles in a safe, supportive environment. As each participant learns that life outside of the support group is no different from life inside it, he experiments with the use of the principles in all aspects of his life. Many participants in existing support groups have successfully transferred their use of the principles to their lives outside of their support groups, thereby allowing their whole world to be a mutual support system.

Suggested Outline for a Typical Support Group Meeting

Start on Time

This encourages the participants to come on time and is respectful of those who do so.

Center the Energy in the Group

Sit in a circle, hold hands, close eyes, and allow the energies of the participants to blend together.

Allow a Leader to Emerge

The centering process creates a peaceful environment that usually inspires one of the participants to offer to lead the group.

Offer the Opportunity to Do the Eleven Steps

Each person announces a number between one and ten. A high number indicates that it is important for that person to have the opportunity to go through the Eleven Steps. More than one person can announce the same number.

Starting with high numbers first, the leader, or other group member, takes each participant who wishes to do so through the Eleven Steps. The participant (the presenter) is free to stop the exercise at any time. It must always be his choice, as the group is there to support the presenter.

It is important to remember that no participant is to suggest a solution to a presenter, either during or after the exercise. Going through the Eleven Steps is the sole method used to deal with the situation being presented. Solutions suggested by others are not helpful. Meaningful change occurs for the presenter only when he gains his own insights to the solution to his problem.

Feeling the unconditional love and support of the group provides the presenter with an environment of safety that encourages him to tell the truth to himself. Each member allows whatever the presenter says to be perfect, whether or not he agrees with his statements. Perceiving the presenter as perfect just the way he is enables the group to feel what unconditional love and support are like.

If the presenter has any difficulty with step 7 of the Eleven Steps (perceive the same situation differently), the leader suggests that the presenter continue with that step at home. The exercise is then continued by proceeding to the next step.

Have Each Participant State His Individual Purpose

The group members feel the statement of purpose with the presenter while it is being stated.

Read the Group Purpose

To arrive at the group purpose, each member separately defines his purpose for the group. The group then jointly composes a single statement of purpose, which incorporates the essential elements proposed by each member. It is helpful to keep the final statement as short and as inspiring as possible. The give-and-take that this procedure requires teaches the participants how to align their energies in support of each other and in support of the group (see chapter 41).

It is important for the final statement to reflect the group's purpose on a feeling level. Any member can suggest a modification of the statement until every member feels inspired when the statement is read.

The group purpose should be read and felt by the entire group at every meeting. When the statement of purpose ceases to feel inspiring, any participant can suggest a further modification so that the statement can again become an inspiration to each member of the group.

Go through the Feeling Exercise

Each person, in turn, closes his eyes, proceeds with the exercise, and when he is finished, opens his eyes as a signal for the next person to begin. After all participants have finished, they hold hands and blend together the heightened awareness of their feelings.

THE FEELING EXERCISE

Close your eyes and scan your body. Notice how you are feeling. Then:

1. Feel the feeling free of any thoughts you have about it.
2. Feel love for the feeling just the way it is.
3. Feel love for yourself having that feeling.

Review a Principle

Read a statement of principle from this book or any other source. Many groups focus on the selected principle until the next meeting.

Make Individual Requests for Specific Support

Each person makes a request for specific support. Remember that all improvement in the quality of one's life takes place in consciousness. The request for support focuses on support in consciousness (see chapter 40). For example, assume that a person is having difficulty in forgiving a friend. The request to the group may be: "I ask for support in consciousness in feeling forgiveness for my friend." Once a person is able to make a clear request for support in consciousness, backed with 100 percent intention, success will follow. The only variable is the willingness of the person requesting the support to sustain the clear intention to achieve the desired result. Asking for the support strengthens the commitment to oneself to achieve the desired result.

Examples of requests for support in consciousness by a person experiencing a shortage of cash flow can be as follows: "I ask for support in consciousness in repeating the definition of abundance in front of the mirror until I feel the abundance of the Universe at a deep feeling level," or "I ask for support in consciousness in continually acknowledging all the abundance I presently have."

Remember that all requests are to be spontaneous and reflect the true desire of the presenter at the moment the request is made.

After the request for specific support is stated, the group responds to the member: "(Grady), we unconditionally love and support you just the way you are in all your magnificence."

Have Each Person Report on Ways in Which Use of the Principles and Requests for Support Have Been Helpful

Do the Positive Reflection Exercise

In this exercise, each member is given the opportunity to see positive qualities in every other member in the group. For a person to observe the positive qualities of another, the observer must have these qualities himself.

EXAMPLE: In looking at one person, you realize he has qualities of gentleness and kindness. In looking at another person, you immediately notice his humor and joyfulness.

The exercise is carried out in the following manner:

Each participant receives a description of his positive qualities from every member of the group, each in turn. Then the next person in the group becomes the recipient. Each person addressing the recipient looks directly into his eyes and says, "The positive qualities I see in you that you reflect to me are:_____." The recipient responds by saying, "Thank you." The exercise continues until every member has had a chance to receive acknowledgments.

This exercise demonstrates the principle behind giving and receiving. When a person gives acknowledgment to another, he is really acknowledging himself. It is a simultaneous gift from the giver to another and from the giver to himself. This is a very powerful exercise. As the members deepen their appreciation for each other, the exercise serves to anchor and expand the depth of their feelings.

Set the Date and Time for the Next Meeting

End the Meeting on Time

43
Surrender

One of the ways we complicate our lives is by thinking of ourselves as separate from each other and from the Universe. So strong is this belief that we must continually remind ourselves that each of us is an integral part of a universal experience and that our individual power derives from this connectedness. The more we open ourselves to the inherent perfection in everything just the way it is, the more fun we have. The easier it becomes for each of us to surrender to the love in ourselves and to the love in everyone else, the richer and fuller is our life experience.

The opportunity to live our lives is the greatest privilege we have. Like any privilege, it must first be cherished in order to be enjoyed. Every time we open our hearts to another, we exercise this privilege and learn again what a magnificent gift our life is.

44
Quiet, Harmony, and Rhythm

There is a basic rhythm to the Universe. And each of us has a rhythm that is in natural harmony with this universal rhythm. There is a rhythm to our walk, to our speech, to our eating, to our playing golf and tennis. There is a rhythm to our relating to others. All of us together have rhythms that are in harmony with each other and with the Universe. Life is so simple when we hear, feel, and follow these rhythms. But we have to be quiet to hear and feel them.

The Infinite Intelligence of the Universe is behind these rhythms. As we become more and more sensitive to them, we pick up the natural guidance that is there for us, at all times.

The world of illusion, with its customary disregard for what is natural, simple, and easy, creates so much background noise that often we do not hear and feel these rhythms. We can choose to create more quiet in our lives in order to hear and feel these basic rhythms. Our increased sensitivity to these rhythms will also attract to us a more peaceful environment in which to live our lives. As a result, we will have a deeper appreciation for the magnificent harmony that is always present in the Universe.

45
Uncovering Joy

If we perceive any part of our lives as less than perfect just the way it is, that is a misperception on our part. Our unwillingness to see the perfection in everything just the way it is blocks the flow of universal energy into us. The decision to keep a misperception alive is a decision to resist the abundance of the Universe in one or more of its many forms.

In addition to increasing our willingness to see the perfection in everything just the way it is, we can focus our attention on the quality of life that we desire. Quality of life is really the feeling that is the setting for the events and people that pass through our lives. If we are feeling wonderful, we don't really care who we are with, where we are, or what is going on.

The underlying feeling that we all have access to is joy. It is a part of our essence. We can keep reminding ourselves of our basic love of joy and of our deep desire to relate to one another in joyful ways. And we can choose to rediscover this inner joy over and over again. Most of us have buried our joy below layers of judgments and repressed feelings. It is helpful to keep peeling the layers off until the joy is uncovered and allowed to fill our being.

There is no substitute for this procedure, and it is a truly personal experience for each of us. We cannot do it for another. All we can do is support a person who is doing it for himself.

The principles discussed in this book are the intellectual justification for believing that our joy is real. Using the principles enables us to release the joy within and experience the fun of allowing it to become an ever-increasing part of our lives.

Of one thing we can be certain: Joy will always be there—in us and in everyone else.

The quality of our lives then depends upon:

1. the degree to which we are willing to recognize that the feeling of joy is real;
2. the degree to which we are willing to release the joy within; and
3. the degree to which we recognize that the only obstacle to releasing joy is our unwillingness to express love for someone or something.

A good way to practice locating joy is to do the Feeling Exercise (see chapter 29). The more we look for, uncover, and get in touch with the joy within, the more real it becomes for us. There is no other way to do this. If we wish to achieve a life of joy, we have to continually practice experiencing joy. The means and the end are always identical. You achieve joy by being joyful.

46
The Three Steps—
A New Dance of Life

Whenever anything occurs that creates discomfort in your body, remind yourself of the following:

1. Whatever you are experiencing is something that the deepest part of you wants you to experience.

2. Feel love for yourself just the way you are, i.e., with the thoughts and feelings you presently have. You cannot be different from the way you are, and you cannot make any mistakes. Whatever you think or feel is to be loved just the way it is. In fact, those precise thoughts and feelings are there just so that you can feel love for yourself having them.

3. It is not helpful to judge anyone, including yourself. If you are judging anyone, you are locking up the love energy within you. To free this love energy, begin the practice of forgiveness. Daily, in the quiet of your room, bring the person you are judging into your consciousness. Feel yourself forgiving him. Continue with this practice on a daily basis until you notice that you have released all judgment and all anger toward that person. When you notice that the judgment and anger are

gone, you can begin to feel deep forgiveness for the person. When you have succeeded in feeling deep forgiveness, you are ready to feel deep love for him. Continue to do this exercise daily until you feel love easily, just at the mention of the person's name. Be patient. Allow as long as you need to comfortably release all judgment and consistently feel love. Do not make time a factor. Be gentle and kind to yourself as you do this.

As you learn to make this three-step procedure a habit, you will recognize how easy it is to improve the quality of your life. You will realize that all that stands between you and a life of increased richness and fullness is your willingness to allow yourself to have it.

47
We Start
from Completion

We cannot enjoy our lives to the fullest unless we are willing to accept everything as perfect just the way it is, and to fully and freely express ourselves in accordance with our talents.

We do not need to earn a life that works perfectly. It is a gift from the Universe. In other words, we start out being whole and complete. Everything is always provided for us. We are without anything that we need only because we believe that we cannot have it at that moment, or more accurately stated, we are not willing to open ourselves to receive it.

Abundance is the natural state of affairs in the Universe. It wants to flow through our lives. When we are not enjoying total abundance in each and every aspect of our lives, it is only because we are pushing it away.

Every time we try to feel better by changing anything in the world around us, we deny the truth that everything is already perfect. Making peace with everything just the way it is allows us to appreciate the fact that each of us is already perfect just the way he is.

Life is always the way we view it. It is a perceptual experience. Perceive it as perfect and it is perfect. Perceive it as anything other than perfect and we attract chaos and pain into our lives.

Happiness is being at peace with what is, opening our hearts to ourselves and each other, and feeling the deep love that is the essence of all that is in this beautiful Universe. Believe it! Enjoy it! And then, you do have it all!

FOR INFORMATION ABOUT SUPPORT GROUPS,
WORKSHOPS, BOOKS AND TAPES

CALL 1-800-476-4785

OR WRITE:
CELEBRATION PUBLISHING
ROUTE 3, BOX 365AA
SYLVA, NC 28779